PENGUIN BOOKS
ROLE MODELS

Shehla Rashid is an academic with research interests in technology and politics. She is also a tech policy consultant, offering expertise on policy matters related to emerging technologies like AI. One of the prominent youth figures in Indian politics and activism, Shehla is the former vice president of the JNU Students' Union (JNUSU) and the first Kashmiri woman to be elected to the position. She cares deeply about the condition of Indian Muslims and hopes to bring a change through her initiatives, such as skill development programmes for the Kashmiri youth.

ADVANCE PRAISE FOR THE BOOK

'This book is a unique and important contribution towards national unity, highlighting how some of India's brightest and best minds are Muslims, contributing tirelessly towards the dream of making India into Viksit Bharat by 2047' —**Kiren Rijiju, Union minister of parliamentary affairs and minority affairs**

'Shehla Rashid's book is a riveting account of the best and brightest Muslim "heroes" in contemporary India. This brilliant work is a must-read! It will be welcomed by everyone in the country who recognizes that celebrating diversity is integral to the idea of India'—**Prof. Amitabh Mattoo, dean, School of International Studies, JNU**

'Shehla Rashid breaks away from negative stereotypes of the community to showcase the lives and work of remarkable individuals whose talent, hard work and wisdom have enriched India. *Role Models* is a must-read for anyone interested in contemporary India'—**Sadanand Dhume, columnist, *Wall Street Journal***

'In *Role Models*, Shehla Rashid provides compelling insights into the lives of Indian Muslims who have made significant contributions to civic life, scientific and professional development and the cultural arts in the country.

'Despite their contribution to the freedom struggle, as well as in the emergence of a national consciousness after independence, contemporary discourse on Indian Muslims has predominantly centred on religion-based identity and communalism. Rashid makes characteristically sharp observations on the vested interests behind the "appeasement politics" that India has witnessed for decades, and how it has reduced an enterprising, diverse and compassionate community into a caricature. Being a trailblazer herself, she shares the angst of many other Indian Muslims who wonder why there isn't more popular discussion on the contributions to public life made by Indian Muslims.

'In writing about the varied lives and journeys of stalwart Indian Muslims such as Nigar Shaji, A.R. Rahman, Lt Gen. Syed Ata Hasnain, Prof. Tariq Mansoor and Dr Jamal Khan, among others, Rashid seeks to do away with the extant negative discourse and instead recognize and celebrate Indian Muslims. She makes it clear that the purpose of writing such a book isn't to "box" these achievers into the category of "Muslim", but to instead revel in the universality of their achievements which every Indian can resonate with.

'The inspiring stories of these noteworthy individuals reflect the positive spirit of progress and integration that Indian Muslims subscribe to, and thus, engenders this compilation with a heartening message for many young Muslims in the country today who seek and are in need of "role models". Rashid's endeavour and objective must be applauded wholeheartedly'—**Hardeep Singh Puri, Union minister of petroleum and natural gas**

'It gives me immense pleasure to endorse this effort by Shehla Rashid to put together the life stories of prominent Indian Muslims, highlighting their contributions to national life. It showcases the diversity and plurality of Indian society. Through the stories presented in it, this book also emphasizes the importance of education, a cause to which I have dedicated my life. As a member of a minority community myself, I strongly endorse the sentiment expressed by various authors in this book that we need to step forth and contribute towards nation-building. We need to pool all efforts—big and small—to build a Viksit Bharat (developed India) by 2047, a dream envisioned by our beloved Prime Minister Shri Narendra Modiji.

'I started the Indian Minorities Foundation with the aim of promoting interfaith harmony and inclusive development. There was a glaring absence of interfaith forums in India, and my team and I felt a need to fill this void. We got immense support and encouragement from PM Modi, who believes in "Sabka Saath, Sabka Vikas" and "Sabka Vishwas". IMF works in the sphere of faith and spirituality, building bridges to promote communal harmony, and is proud to have supported this book and its aims of building bridges, reducing othering, and fostering empathy by presenting relatable life stories of Indian Muslim achievers.

'I'm honoured to be among the first ones to review this book and it shows the fine intellectual bearings of the author's young mind, which will take our nation forward. Through this book, Shehla hopes to move the discourse beyond political and religious narratives and promote the idea of a reform-oriented "Muslim civil society", an interesting and fresh concept. I wish her all the best and hope that this book makes its intended contribution by taking us towards a Viksit Bharat by 2047. Jai Hind!'—**Satnam Singh Sandhu, member (nominated), Rajya Sabha, chancellor of Chandigarh University and founder of Indian Minorities Foundation**

ROLE MODELS

Inspiring Stories of Indian Muslim Achievers

SHEHLA RASHID

PENGUIN BOOKS

An imprint of Penguin Random House

PENGUIN BOOKS

Penguin Books is an imprint of the Penguin Random House group of companies
whose addresses can be found at global.penguinrandomhouse.com

Published by Penguin Random House India Pvt. Ltd
4th Floor, Capital Tower 1, MG Road,
Gurugram 122 002, Haryana, India

Penguin
Random House
India

First published in Penguin Books by Penguin Random House India 2024

ISBN 9780143470922

Typeset in Sabon LT Std by Manipal Technologies Limited, Manipal
Printed at Thomson Press India Ltd, New Delhi

www.penguin.co.in

MIX
Paper | Supporting
responsible forestry
FSC® C010615

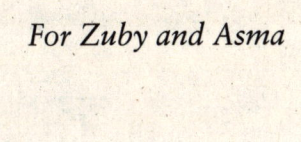
For Zuby and Asma

Contents

Foreword   xi

Introduction   xxi

Embody the Change You Want to See   1
—*A.R. Rahman*

The Sky Is No Longer the Limit for India   18
—*Nigar Shaji*

On Grand Slams, Girl Power and Building a
Better India   31
—*Sania Mirza*

Hard Work Is Its Own Reward   43
—*Huma Qureshi*

So, What's Your Excuse?   55
—*Shams Aalam*

Going the Last Mile   75
—*Dr Jamal A. Khan*

Let the Amrit Kaal Be a Buildathon   99
—Dr Zahir Kazi

Reflections of a Diplomat   113
—Dr Ausaf Sayeed

Bridging Worlds: My Journey as an Indian
Muslim Scholar in International Relations   134
—Dr Sana Hashmi

A People's General   150
—Lt Gen. Syed Ata Hasnain

Faith in Constitutional Ideas Is the Only Way Out   174
—Prof. Faizan Mustafa

Why Prime Minister Narendra Modi Is My
Role Model   196
—Prof. Tariq Mansoor

For the Love of the Land   206
—Asif Bhamla

Change Doesn't Stop Because a Theory Says
It Is Impossible   216
—Shehla Rashid

Perspectives on Deprivation, Victimhood
Narrative, Isolationism and Radicalization   242
—Amana Begam Ansari

Acknowledgements   261
Appendix   267
Notes   275

Foreword

When Shehla approached me to write a chapter on my life for this book, I told her that every detail of my life has been written about so extensively that, at times, even I'm not aware of certain details that people seem to know about me! When you have been in the public eye for as long as I have, there isn't an aspect of your life that is left unscrutinized, or an area left uninterrogated. However, I do share her interest in promoting role models for younger people in various professions, so I decided to lend my voice to this project. The main aim of this book is to inspire younger people to achieve professional success. I believe that the most important factor for success is choosing the right profession or specialization. It is difficult to achieve excellence without being genuinely interested in your field. I would like to express this using a simple one-liner: 'to be interesting, you have to be interested' attributed variously to David Ogilvy, Dale Carnegie, and others. If you lack interest, passion or drive, it is unlikely that you will create something great.

Who can be a better protagonist of this advice than me, seeing as I started out as an actor and failed miserably? Though I got work as an actor, I did not get either satisfaction or recognition. It is only through a process of trial and error that I ended up screenwriting, which is where I achieved greatness, recognition, professional satisfaction and fame, defining the shape of modern Indian cinema through my characters and the Hindi 'masala' film blockbuster format. There isn't a career path that I haven't tried out. I took the civil services exam, I am a trained pilot, I excelled in cricket and I acted in twenty-five films before finding my true calling: screenwriting. Therefore, the role of parents today is to help children find their niche, their true area(s) of interest, not to lay down the choice of career for their kids.

Next comes the matter of honing your skills and cultivating your interest. To share an anecdote with you, there is a small library in Mahim—one of the few to have stood the travails of time—from which I would borrow books back in the day when purchasing books was not within everyone's reach. Borrowing too came with strict rules. You had to return the book within twenty-four hours, or you would be fined. This ensured that we actually read the books, as opposed to the status of décor that they have been relegated to today. So, I would read extensively, immersing myself in books.

On one occasion, while I was still a struggling actor, I went to the library to borrow a new book, only to be told by the librarian that I had already read every title in the library and that they had no new books to lend me! My success as a writer is due in large part to my devotion to reading. So, my advice to younger writers is that in order to be a good writer, you have to be a good reader. In order to be a good leader, you have to be a good follower. In order to be a successful prince, you must be a good warrior. Unless you go through the grind in your chosen area, you won't achieve greatness. Every child is born with potential, but it is through practice, hard work, sincerity and investment that we can hone that potential.

Shehla also asked me to reflect on my struggles as a young person. One of the biggest voids in my life is that both my parents passed away by the time I turned fourteen. My mother had tuberculosis, so we weren't allowed to go near her or hug her. This is before TB became a fully curable illness. On one occasion, when I greeted her from a distance as she sat in the sun, she failed to recognize me, so prolonged was our separation! When the nurse attending to her identified me as young Salim, she broke down, and I was at a loss to understand why, too young to make sense of complex emotions at the tender age of eight.

Though my family was wealthy, I was determined to make it on my own, choosing not to fall back on family wealth. So, I rented half a room in Marina

Guest House, Bandra, as a struggling young actor, and my biggest aspiration at the time was to be able to rent the full room because the snoring of my ever-changing roommates was unbearable. No sooner had I gotten used to one style of snoring than the style would change, and I had to get used to a new tune. What can be a bigger struggle than this!

I'll spare you the minute details of my professional struggles, as you can read them on Wikipedia or in the countless magazine articles written about me. But I want to stress the importance of patience and focus in life—whether as individuals or as a community. We need *sabr* (patience). We need to patiently build our own character, personality, skills and competencies. The fact that we may not be getting ahead in life as quickly as we would like to shouldn't deter us from working hard.

We must find motivation within ourselves by visualizing where we want to be in life. For me, that visualization involved being the full occupant of my rented room at Marina Guest House, working towards which propelled me to success! Someone else may visualize being an astronaut, a singer or a leader. No dream is big or small. It is how we achieve our goals—the means that we use—that shapes our character. Handling success is not everyone's cup of tea either. Success has destroyed more people than failure has. Therefore, it is important to be grounded and to build one's character along the way.

Fear of failure or desire for quick success should not lead us to take shortcuts, as the only path to true success is the slow one. Failure is an important milestone on the path to success. Therefore, only those who do not fear failure can achieve true success. To my mind, one such figure is the legendary actor, director and producer late Dev Anand sahab, who made one flop movie after the other without getting affected by failure in the slightest! In fact, no sooner had one movie flopped than he would jump on to the next project. No wonder he is considered one of the greatest actors in the history of Indian cinema.

The moral of the story is that we must focus on perfecting our craft with sincerity and not worry about the outcome. Success comes in its own sweet time, but we must first put in our best efforts and improve ourselves as much as possible. Whether you aspire to join the civil service or to be an actor, the formula for success is perseverance. The quote, 'A master has failed more times than a beginner has even tried' by Stephen McCranie, sums up the recipe for mastery and finesse in any craft.

In our Indian tradition, the goddess Lakshmi represents riches, while Saraswati represents art, wisdom, knowledge, etc. The gift of Lakshmi comes and goes, but what remains with us is our talent, skill and expertise, which come from recognizing, developing and sharpening Ma Saraswati's gift. Your mastery of your craft is something that no one can take away from you. While some people are naturally gifted with a good voice, others are great at coding, accounting, writing, dancing, cooking and so on. Success in life requires recognizing our gift and developing it through education, learning, practice and devotion. *Vardhans* (gifts) that are not cultivated won't grow. Even someone like Late Lata Mangeshkar ji would practise her singing intensively, putting in several hours of *riyaaz* (practice) daily, never once taking her success for granted.

Art is nurtured in solitude and exhibited in public. You cannot be constantly on the move while writing a song or a screenplay. You will need to set aside time and space, minimize distractions and maximize focus. To this day, I use a feature phone in order to avoid distraction and stay focused on developing my craft. Even in today's age, we can develop focus by meditating or by praying slowly with solemnity and mindfulness, without pomp and show, and with meaning. Sometimes, we are so focused on distractions that we do not feel in touch with our prayers! Even the act of prayer today is publicized on social media, becoming a matter of likes and reposts. Today, we have communal clashes on the pretext of slogans being chanted outside a mosque. So what, if someone chants slogans outside a mosque? If we were really focused on prayer, we wouldn't mind what was going on outside.

Our relationship with God should be deeply personal and based on love rather than fear. We must learn forgiveness from the Exalted Prophet (PBUH) himself. He forgave even those who threw garbage at him. Who are we to give a call to behead someone on the basis of something that they said? We may express our displeasure or say, 'God bless you' to such people whose hearts bear so much hatred as to abuse others, but we must not descend into anarchy ourselves. At the same time, we must respect other religions too.

Religion, however, is not the only pretext that we use for our petty fights. Looking at the number of road rage incidents, fights over parking and incessant honking at one another shows how much we Indians need to evolve as a society. It is not important to succeed only professionally. We must first become good people and good citizens. India is on the cusp of greatness, but it requires citizens to rise above petty differences and work collectively for the greater good. Once we see ourselves as Indians first and unite for a common cause, the smaller differences can be worked upon.

One of our biggest misconceptions is that an individual can't change anything on his or her own. I disagree with this view because history bears witness that it is individuals who formulate a vision, inspire and lead people. Be it Jesus, Mohammed (PBUH), Martin Luther King, Nelson Mandela, M.K. Gandhi or anyone else, individuals shape societies and cultures. When I went to the cinema hall to watch Richard Attenborough's movie *Gandhi*, I felt changed as a person. I wasn't the same person while climbing down the stairs from the exit as I had been while climbing the stairs from the other side! Such is the power of role models, and that is why the stories of achievers need to be told and read.

Individual effort and perseverance alter the course of history. If each person believes that his or her individual effort will amount to nothing, then no one will ever put in any effort at all. However, if everyone works in a common direction, believing in a common cause, individual effort can be channelled towards nation-building. That is why Prime Minister Narendra Modi has issued a bold call to all of us to do our personal best in order to make our country a *Viksit Bharat* (developed India) by 2047 – marking 100 years of our independence from the British rule. India has suffered a lot due to the devastating impact of the colonial rule, and now we must rise up with ambition and resolve. We, as citizens, need to leave behind our differences and unite for the cause of nation-building, towards this mission.

Each one of us must contribute to this vision in whatever way possible—no contribution is big or small. Our combined efforts will matter, provided we work in a common direction. By presenting stories of inspiring individuals this book seeks to inspire younger Indians to achieve success which in turn will contribute to national development. Each individual and each community must contribute to this dream, only then will development be inclusive. Indian Muslims, like everyone else, must own this dream and participate in this vision with vigour and optimism. Instead of unproductive fixations on our differences, we as Indians need to think about how to excel professionally and be kind to one another, for the sake of our motherland.

I want to conclude with a few lines from the timeless classic 'Jeena Isi Ka Naam Hai' starring Raj Kapoor sahab to remind us of our purpose in life: love and kindness.

Kisi ki muskurahaton pe ho nisar
Kisi ka dard mil sake to le udhaar
Kisi ke waaste ho tere dil mein pyaar
Jeena isi ka naam hai
Mite jo pyar ke liye woh zindagi, jale bahar ke liye woh zindagi
kisi ko ho naa ho hame toh aitbar, jeena isika nam hai.

These lyrics by Shailendra not only capture the purpose of human existence but also the power of individual effort and the power of small, everyday acts of kindness. I wish this book success, and I hope that it achieves its goal of inspiring younger Indians for hard work, excellence, kindness, mutual harmony and success.

Salim Khan,
January 2024
Bandra, Mumbai

Introduction

This book highlights the contributions of Indian Muslims to civic national life by presenting the life stories and work of achievers such as Nigar Shaji, programme director of low earth orbit missions at Indian Space Research Organisation (ISRO) and project director of the Aditya L-1 solar exploration mission; globally renowned music composer and reticent genius A.R. Rahman; tennis ace Sania Mirza; Padma Shri awardee Dr Zahir Kazi; actor, producer and author Huma Qureshi; military leader Lt Gen. Syed Ata Hasnain; former ambassador of India to Saudi Arabia and Yemen, Dr Ausaf Sayeed; former vice chancellor of Aligarh Muslim University (AMU), Prof. Tariq Mansoor; former vice chancellor of National Academy of Legal Studies and Research (NALSAR), Prof. Faizan Mustafa and the pioneer of dendritic cell immunotherapy in India, Dr Jamal Khan, among others. This book is rare in that it provides detailed insight into their lives for the first time.

Whether you are a music lover, a follower of astronomy, passionate about medicine, a sports enthusiast, a foreign policy buff, a film aficionado or someone who cares about environmental issues or politics, you will enjoy reading the essays in this book. We have seen many negative media portrayals of Muslims, and this book attempts to humanize the discourse about Muslims by presenting inspiring life stories that everyone can relate to. While we are somewhat aware of the contributions and sacrifices made by Indian Muslims during the freedom struggle, highlighting the work of notable Muslims in contemporary India was a long-overdue task.

When I approached a long list of Muslim achievers to contribute autobiographical essays to this book, I received enthusiastic responses from them, because, surprisingly, there exists no book highlighting the achievements of living Indian Muslims. Barring the ones on foreign policy, most of the chapters are based on detailed personal interviews which were subsequently faithfully woven into readable, relatable autobiographical essays in consultation with the contributors. Some of the shorter interviews are reproduced as such. The contributors were asked to reflect on their life, career, struggles, motivation, contributions and message for the youth. They were also asked to reflect on the role of Indian Muslims in civic national life and how we can contribute to the dream of building a Viksit Bharat (developed India) by 2047.

While former President of India, the late Dr A.P.J. Abdul Kalam, gave us Vision 2020 for India, Prime Minister Narendra Modi has energized us again with the mission of building a Viksit Bharat by 2047. The pursuit of a Viksit Bharat will require a mindset shift among Indians irrespective of faith. Prof. Faizan Mustafa, in his essay, reminds us that Article 51A of the Constitution of India makes it every citizen's fundamental duty to strive for excellence. In striving for excellence, we uplift ourselves, our communities and our nation. So, I put together this book in the hope that the life stories of these inspiring individuals will infuse a positive spirit among readers, especially the youth, and motivate them to strive for excellence and success.

Sociologically speaking, role models can positively impact the motivation for 'status attainment' (i.e., success) among younger individuals of a social group by shaping their aspirational matrix. The term 'role model' was first coined in the 1940s by the renowned American sociologist Robert K. Merton, who posited that individuals compare themselves with 'reference groups'—social categories they aspire to belong to—adopting their behaviours and values.[1] Building on this, Albert Bandura's social learning theory emphasized the importance of observational learning, where individuals acquire new behaviours and attitudes simply by observing others.[2]

The sociological interest in role models stems from their potential to drive upward mobility amongst

members of their community, often a minority.[3]
There are three ways in which role models can inspire
behaviours that lead to upward mobility of status
aspirants: 'a) by acting as behavioural models, b) by
representing the possible, and c) by being inspirational[4].'
Therefore, while soliciting contributions to this book,
I asked the contributors to focus on these behavioural
aspects, elaborating on how they overcame difficulties
and how they stayed motivated through failure or
hardship. If you had to read only one essay from this
book, I would recommend the one by para-swimmer
Shams Aalam, whose story I find most inspiring and
whose attitude to life is uplifting.

This book boasts of a fair gender balance - a World
no. 1 athlete, an aerospace engineer, a foreign policy
professional and a movie star - this book shows that
no dream is too big for women. The stories of Nigar
Shaji, Huma Qureshi and Sania Mirza show how far
confidence, self-belief and familial support can take us,
as women. When a woman goes to work, the net worth
of her family is doubled. Replicate this at a community
level, and we can double our economic power simply
by unlocking the full potential of women.

While this book contains the life stories of a select
few achievers, it must be mentioned that there is a
vast majority of Muslims, which silently makes its
contributions to various professions—civil services,
fashion design, customer support, film direction,
medicine, philanthropy and so on—making us proud.

Finally, there are millions of Muslims engaged in informal employment in both organized and unorganized sectors—drivers, gig workers, delivery partners, farmers, etc.—who power the economy, making life in India incredibly convenient and increasingly making our country a preferred destination for tourism, business, and investment. We should be equally proud of them. All of them, whether rich or poor, skilled or semi-skilled, are an essential component of Brand India, which is premised on the power of youth, skills, innovation, a positive outlook, a growth mindset and hard work.

The unfortunate use of the term *puncturewallas*** ('puncture mechanic') on social media as an insult for poor, hardworking Muslims has permeated our discourse. But it is puncturewallas who ensure that there isn't a stranded woman anywhere in the country without recourse to assistance! We are proud of our contributions, whether big or small, and we are proud of our country despite its problems.

While it is surprising that no volume on the contributions of contemporary Muslim public figures exists, it is also unsurprising because it wouldn't make sense for them to over-emphasize their identity for fear of being boxed as 'Muslim' professionals when they are otherwise universally celebrated. Most of the

---

*A term intended as a putdown, based on the stereotype that mechanics who mend punctured tyres are predominantly Muslim.

people featured in this book admitted that they have not been looked at as anything but professionals. They are unanimous in asserting that they have never been profiled as Muslims because—and all of them agree on this point—once you achieve a certain level of professional expertise, knowledge or success, you transcend the categories of identity, gaining everyone's respect and becoming a role model for all.

Be it Salim Khan, Sania Mirza, A.R. Rahman, Ata Hasnain, Huma Qureshi or Dr Jamal Khan—all of them emphatically voiced the sentiment that their non-Muslim brethren have been their collaborators, mentors, colleagues, supporters and team members who have cheered them on and watched them grow. I'm grateful that all of them, despite their usual reticence, agreed to come on board, recognizing the growing need for a fresh discourse about Muslims and for narrative reform within the Muslim community.

The need for narrative and discursive reform stems from the fact that existing parables are unhelpful. The Sachar Committee Report (SCR) in 2006 flagged the socio–economic and educational conditions of Indian Muslims as being worse off or only marginally better than those of some of the constitutionally protected sections of society, stating that Indian Muslims lag behind on various human development indicators.[5] The SCR also flagged that Muslims fare worst in terms of regular employment among all socio-religious groups.[6] As per the Census 2011, the illiteracy rate among Muslims was 42 per cent whereas only 2.7 per cent Muslims had an education level of graduate or above.[7] As per the 2021-22 report of the All India Survey on Higher Education (AISHE), 21.1 lakh (2.1 million) Muslims were enrolled in higher education[8]. Relative to our population of 20 crore (200 million), this is a mere 1 per cent! We must ask ourselves how we got here. Despite accusations of 'appeasement' by previous governments, how did we remain so backward? I'll attempt to explain this strange paradox in simple terms.

Basically, what is termed 'appeasement' was often tokenism masquerading as affirmative action. What passed off as 'secularism' was often a free pass for injustices such as denial of married women's rights under the guise of 'personal law', misuse of Waqf assets[9], and so on. Paying lip service to the rather elusive cause of 'secularism' has done no good to the community at large, as the numbers show, and has only served to create a protectorate of vices where malpractices were tolerated. Conversely, this also meant that the political parties at the helm too got a free pass for various commissions and omissions, such as their failure to maintain law and order and rein in communal violence, as long as they left this protectorate of vices untouched. The very parties that oversaw numerous communal clashes seek votes in the name of secularism and we throng to them for no more than comforting words.

We, as a community, have been so preoccupied with whatever this 'secularism' entails that we are content with not having basic development, civic amenities, access to healthcare and sanitation, etc.[10] What's worse is that such lip service and tokenism give off an impression of appeasement, making the majority community believe that minorities are getting special treatment! The purported 'appeasement' has resulted in no more than self-proclaimed 'secular' governments failing to regulate or reform both the Muslim private sphere (such as denial of Muslim women's matrimonial rights) as well as the Muslim public sphere (such as squandering and misuse of Waqf assets). This has delayed requisite reforms within the community, keeping Indian Muslims backward. Governments must understand that the pursuit of a Viksit Bharat cannot afford to leave behind 200 million Muslims.

However, while we look to governments to explain our condition, we must also look within. We allow all this to happen because we are preoccupied with *akhirat* (other-worldly concerns), while our faith clearly calls for balancing akhirat with *duniya* (this-worldly concerns). This hierarchy—where other-worldly pursuits are ranked above this-worldly outcomes— also defines who our role models are. The founder of AMU, Sir Syed Ahmed Khan, was at the receiving end of numerous fatwas for his modernist views.[11] While most Indians, irrespective of faith, pay tributes to the

11th President of India, Late Dr A.P.J. Abdul Kalam, and consider him a role model, the discussions that we hear in our community pertain to the status of his faith—whether he was *really* a Muslim or not—owing to his pluralist views.[12]

It was none other than the face of Muslim politics in India, Dr. Rafiq Zakaria, who kicked off the debate about Dr. Kalam's Muslimness in an article titled 'What is Muslim about Kalam?' published in *Asian Age*.[13] It shows the poverty of civic discourse among Muslims that we are unlikely to discuss Dr. Kalam's ideas, or his work at ISRO, or even how he overcame immense personal grief to complete the mission to launch ISRO's Space Launch Vehicle (SLV)-3.[14] Instead, we debate the status of his faith.

Even as late as 2020, five years after his death, an article by a Muslim writer in *Outlook* magazine lamented the imposition of Dr Kalam as a hero upon Muslims because the latter was neither a martyr like Safdar Hashmi nor jailed for violence like Bhagat Singh.[15] In other words, a good Muslim was either a martyred Muslim or an incarcerated one, but never someone who was conventionally successful! This comes from a certain fascination with martyrdom and rebellion, reflecting not only a lack of role models who have achieved this-worldly success but also a contempt for this-worldly outcomes.

This tendency is not limited to Indian Muslims alone. The first Muslim to win the Nobel Prize, renowned

Pakistani nuclear physicist, Professor Abdus Salam, was not even allowed to attend his own felicitation ceremony, following protests by Jamaat-e-Islami, in his home country Pakistan which should have celebrated him.[16] Rather than his pioneering work in Physics, he was judged for being an Ahmadi—a fact that was marginal to his work—and hounded out of Pakistan! This wasn't the case with, say, Sir Albert Einstein whose Jewishness was never questioned despite his rationalist views, who was never ostracized by his community and who was even offered the Presidency of Israel, in recognition of his work. Even after he turned down this offer, he did not face backlash from within his community.

Political and religious preoccupations pervade the Muslim community and there is a glaring absence of what could be thought of as a Muslim civil society (a public sphere outside of state and clergy), leading to a lack of aspirational standards. As per the SCR, a major reason for low educational attainment among Indian Muslims is the perceived lack of returns from education.[17] This means that we do not even enter the race due to our inability to summon the self-belief to dream. We can change this by owning and honouring our achievers, showcasing role models from various fields to spark ambition among younger Muslims and encourage them to dream. My book addresses this need, showing that Muslims are (and can be) among the top achievers in some crucial areas of civic national life. We do not hear about them, because a positive account neither suits those who wish to perpetuate perennial cynicism and victimhood among Muslims, nor does it benefit those who would like to portray Muslims in a bad light.

The lack of role models from within the community (usually a minoritized community) can hinder the community's progress. Seeing someone from their background, or facing similar struggles, succeed can be a powerful motivator, particularly for marginalized or underrepresented groups. Without such figures, feelings of hopelessness and self-doubt might increase. Young people might struggle to develop a positive sense of self if they do not see anyone like themselves achieving success or contributing meaningfully to society. There are three main groups of 'significant others'* who influence our aspirational matrix:

1. **Primary Socializers**: individuals who interact with us most frequently during our early lives, such as parents, caregivers and siblings.
2. **Role Models**: individuals we admire and aspire to emulate. They can be people we know personally, famous figures or even fictional characters.
3. **Reference Groups**: groups or classes of people with whom we identify or wish to identify.

---

*In sociology, the term 'significant other' describes any person or persons with a strong influence on an individual's self-concept

Role models expose individuals to diverse career paths and possibilities. Without them, people might limit their aspirations to what they see around them, potentially overlooking opportunities they never considered, or thought were possible for them. Hence, I have tried my best to include role models from a diverse array of professions.

This book attempts to give visibility to the hardworking Muslim who is paying taxes, contributing to the GDP, bringing India laurels, formulating policy, creating great films, winning medals, Grand Slam titles and Oscars for the country, overseeing space programmes, bringing about innovation in cancer treatment, practising philanthropy and generally being awesome. I want to showcase the diversity of our contributions as well as the diversity of our concerns. I want us to engage with the state as citizens. That's my idea of a development-oriented 'Muslim civil society' which is capable of deliberating upon a variety of issues without being driven by groupthink. After all, we share the same concerns as our non-Muslim neighbours and fellow constituents.

If the roads are bad, we must agitate alongside our fellow citizens. But if our neighbourhoods get a facelift, we must acknowledge the same without hesitation. The way our fellow citizens share a love–hate relationship with political parties, we too must have a love–hate relationship with parties, not as a block but as individual constituents—that's the sign of being rational, thinking individuals in a democracy. Having a perennially adverse relationship with one party or being unquestioningly beholden to another absolves both the parties of any responsibility for our real development.

As Indian citizens, we must assess each candidate in our constituencies and decide who is best for our area. Yet, regardless of who wins, we must also accept the democratic mandate and engage with the state like all other citizens do. There is no need for Muslims to be deemed permanent adversaries of the state. India is an open society where everyone can progress, and we don't need to wait for some messiah in order to succeed. There are enough stories of achievers from humble backgrounds who have succeeded against all odds. Nobody is going to hand us success on a platter. And if there aren't enough pull factors, we must create a push factor by investing so heavily in our skills and personal development that we become indispensable.

Everyone everywhere has faced discrimination in one way or another. We are neither unique in facing discrimination, nor are we guiltless when it comes to discriminating against others and against our own. The only antidote to discrimination is a mix of hard work, perseverance and strong will, which elevates us to our full potential as humans. As *homo sapiens*, we have elevated ourselves from being helpless against nature to being the most successful species, not by complaining about the unfairness of natural events, but by improving our standards of living through ingenuity and the full utilization of our mental faculties. Complaining perennially means that we are operating far below our human potential. The human condition consists in using our mental abilities to conquer and rise up against all odds.

We are in charge of our own destinies to a fairly large extent. The choices that we make as individuals, families or communities determine our progress more than any government intervention can, and the stories in this book illustrate that fact. Most readers will be able to relate to the challenges that these achievers have faced and overcome through perseverance, hard work and resilience. In fact, what is brought out by most of the autobiographical accounts is that adversity should be taken as a test, as it shapes our values, forges us as individuals and prepares us for life. In many ways, therefore, this is a self-help book too!

Just as individuals defeat the odds stacked up against them, countries do too! The essays on foreign policy highlight how India, despite being a third world country, is emerging as a global leader, forging strategic alliances and playing a more proactive role on the world stage. Dr Ausaf Sayeed, former ambassador of India to Saudi Arabia and Yemen talks about the increasing importance of Indian soft power in the Arab world. He presents an insider's view of India's evolving relationship with the region, which can be an enigma for those who observe it from the outside.

A ringside view of India's foreign policy landscape is also brought in by Dr Sana Hashmi, who was once described to me as the 'go-to person for all things India-Taiwan' by a New-Delhi based Taiwanese diplomat. A stereotype-smasher, she is a foreign policy professional working in Taipei. Her essay captures the churn in international relations in the face of an assertive China, and India's role in this emerging order. Her story also demonstrates the diversity of career paths available to younger people today as India expands its diplomatic footprint under the 'Modi–Jaishankar duo'.

Dr Jamal Khan and Huma Qureshi draw our attention to an important facet of professional life by debunking the myth that once you work hard and achieve something, life will be a cakewalk. They bring in a reality check, stressing that work only gets more challenging, albeit more exciting and rewarding. Once you get an A, you can only aspire for an A+. Once you achieve something unique, you are in a league of your own, competing only with yourself. Huma Qureshi also brings in the interesting concept of 'cumulative hard work', which hugely resonated with me.

A word of caution: at times, parents tend to use stories of achievers as a yardstick to berate their children, imposing their own unrealistic expectations on the latter. An important fact about some of the contributors to this book is that they **did not start**

out as achievers or brilliant students at school. They were mediocre—even bad—in the very areas that later became their calling. There is no better teacher than failure, and parents must allow their kids to fail in order to discover the true recipe for success.

Of course, parents have a role as significant others to create a positive environment for their kids and to set standards and goals, even ambitious ones, but these must be balanced with love, encouragement, and by providing solace in failure rather than contempt. Prof. Faizan Mustafa recalls in his essay, Prime Minister Narendra Modi's assertion that Indian parents often tend to use children's report cards as their visiting cards. While it is important to take pride in children's achievements, it is also important to be supportive in failure. Children with neurodivergent traits require additional support and creative learning methods. Often following non-typical paths to 'success', they tend to excel in different ways, bringing in unique ways of thinking and contributing to their work.

We often hear stories of young lives being abruptly ended due to pressures of performance and socially defined standards of success such as percentage and rank. This book is not meant to be yet another template for kids to follow blindly or for parents to impose upon their children, but to present the diversity of career paths available to youth today, beyond medicine and civil services. A genius is not someone who scores an

A+, but one who excels in one's own field, bringing original contributions to it.

Prime Minister Narendra Modi deserves credit for initiating this much-needed dialogue with young children through initiatives such as '*Pariksha Pe Charcha*' (dialogue on examinations), his book *Exam Warriors*, his podcast *Mann Ki Baat* (speaking from the heart), etc., telling young people that not all is lost if you flunk a subject or fail a class. It is okay to take career breaks to figure out your calling, your niche, the area where you are naturally inclined to excel. Failure, setbacks, struggles and hardship are necessary components of success. Hence, this book is as much about failure as it is about success. Behind every success story, there is nearly a decade of ups and downs, invisible hard work and perseverance—be it any profession.

My essay titled 'Change doesn't stop because a theory says it is impossible,' highlights the importance of doing everything with passion and sincerity and of striving to be the best in one's field, be it politics, academia or literature. It highlights the importance of learning from failure and setbacks, engaging in original thinking and rational inquiry, and contributing something new. Politics (or activism, more broadly) is not a conventional career path, though it is glamorous and aspirational, yet the recipe for success is the same as in any other field. What one brings to one's craft or practice is important—*that* is what becomes our legacy. In other words, it's what we contribute to our field that defines us, not the profession we choose.

Speaking of unconventional professions and activism, one of the contributors to this book, the Page Three environmentalist Asif Bhamla, draws on indigenous traditions of Islam to advocate for environmental conservation and moderation. He also hails India's environmental leadership on the global stage under Prime Minister Narendra Modi. He also argues that the Modi government's policies are helping expedite reforms within the Muslim community, thus offering us an opportunity to better ourselves and improve our condition. In his speech at the Sadbhavna programme organized by the Indian Minorities Foundation in Mumbai in 2023, he highlighted how Muslim women used to attract a triple talaq (divorce) for as little as serving bland food! All of us within the community knew this all along, but we would always shy away from saying it out loud. Most of the contributors to this book—and even those who did not end up contributing—have emphasized the need for us, as a community, to proactively initiate reform and embrace progress.

Amana Begum Ansari, who is a columnist, podcaster and research scholar has explained the cyclical relationship among victimhood narratives, isolationism and radicalization that keeps us backward. She explains how socio–economic backwardness feeds our persecution complex, discouraging us from participating in national progress, furthering our socio–economic backwardness and thereby completing the cycle. She proposes a way forward through inclusive development, offering suggestions for socio–economic development of Muslims, especially Pasmanda (backward) Muslims.* After all, we cannot talk about the upliftment of Indian Muslims without addressing the issues faced by the bulk of the community—the Pasmandas. This point is brought out by Prof. Tariq Mansoor's essay too.

Finally, many of the contributors—A.R. Rahman, Prof. Faizan Mustafa, Dr Zahir Kazi and Sania Mirza—have expressed or hinted at the need for private initiative, which includes both individual and community initiatives and institution-building through the spirit of voluntarism and private enterprise. Great nations are not simply built on government doles but on private efforts by the citizenry. We must not always look to governments for reform and initiative.

The SCR pointed out that Waqf† properties could easily generate annual returns to the tune

---

* 'Pasmanda' (those left behind) is a term loosely used to refer to Muslims belonging to the governmental category of Other Backward Classes (OBC) which includes socially and educationally backward castes.
† 'Waqf' (Islamic endowment in perpetuity) denotes a system of Islamic commons which may be leveraged for religious or charitable purposes. Waqf assets (Auqaf) can't be alienated, disposed of, or sold. However, widespread misuse has reduced Waqf in India to a shadow of its potential.

of ₹12,000 crore (a conservative estimate) which can be used to build institutions, especially for the educational upliftment of Muslims.[18] We have been unable to realise this potential as a community due to the gross mismanagement of Auqaf, alienation of Waqf properties and disinterested and incompetent management, ensuring annual losses in revenue amounting to no less than Rs 11,800 crore annually.[19] The prestigious Jamia Hamdard University in Delhi is an example of a well-managed Waqf asset, but such examples are few and far between.

To conclude, we need to think beyond minority institutions which often tend to nurture complacency by shielding us from competition. We can aspire to build centres of excellence that go beyond the minority mindset. The impact of a company such as Wipro, founded by the visionary M.H. Hasham Premji in 1945, is universal, and not limited to the Muslim community alone. His son, Azim Premji, irrevocably donated most of his wealth for philanthropic purposes and created the Azim Premji Foundation (APF) which is valued at $29 billion[20]. The Azim Premji University, founded by the APF, is an aspirational educational institution, creating value for all.*

We must not limit our imagination or see ourselves within the narrow confines of identity. We must

---

*The author has no affiliation whatsoever with any of the aforementioned institutions, and has no conflict of interest to report.

build institutions that foster innovation and nurture excellence, build businesses that are governed well and educational institutions that are run efficiently. We need to get out of the minority mindset and aspire to lead and be at the top. We need to summon the self-belief to dream and never consider ourselves incapable of big things. The inspiring essays presented in this book tell stories of people with such a mindset, which is what it takes to be a role model. I hope that this book will energize readers and fellow citizens to achieve their personal best, which will in turn take us closer to the dream of building a Viksit Bharat by 2047.

Embody the Change You Want to See

—A.R. Rahman

- A.R. Rahman is a globally renowned music composer who has won six National Film Awards, two Academy Awards (Oscars), two Grammy Awards, a BAFTA Award, a Golden Globe Award, fifteen Filmfare Awards and seventeen Filmfare Awards South.
- He was on *TIME* magazine's list of the 100 most influential people in the world. He has been conferred with the Padma Bhushan, India's third-highest civilian award.
- Rahman's genius lies in his seamless blending of influences. He effortlessly incorporates elements of Indian classical music, Carnatic traditions, western electronica and even Sufi devotional

chants. He has composed music for Hollywood films, collaborated with international artists and performed on global stages. His music has become a bridge between cultures, showcasing the richness and diversity of Indian music around the world.

- Also known as '*isai puyal*' (musical storm), the musical genius was honoured by Stanford University for his contributions to global music. He was awarded an honorary doctorate from Berklee College of Music as well as from AMU. He is a household name in India.

- Rahman's embrace of technology has been instrumental in shaping his sound. He was one of the first Indian composers to experiment with digital audio workstations and synthesizers, creating soundscapes that were previously unimaginable. Recently, he pioneered the use of AI in music by recreating the voices of two deceased singers, the late Shahul Hameed and Bamba Bakya, for the song *Thimiri Yezhuda* for the movie *Lal Salaam*.

- He is the founder of the K.M. Music Conservatory, Chennai—a higher education institution that offers a range of part-time and full-time courses in Hindustani, western classical music and music technology.

- He also founded the Firdaus Orchestra—a world-class music studio in Dubai.

Being talented is a gift from God, but being successful is about nurturing God's gift with your own labour. No matter how hard I work, I will never have a voice as sweet as my daughter Khatija's, for instance! However, success requires recognizing your own unique talent and aiming to achieve excellence in your field. God has given something or the other to each one of us, and we must nurture our talents with hard work and passion. In order to distinguish yourself in any field, you must find what is missing and work towards contributing that. Embody the change you want to see in the world. Fill the gap that you perceive exists. Bring to the table what is missing. Do what needs to be done. Ask original questions. When you contribute something original, you are not competing with anyone else. Natural abilities alone cannot explain greatness. One may have a great voice but cannot become a singer without practice. One may have great imagination or humming abilities, but learning how to play a musical instrument is a task as technical as an engineering course. What determines success is the effort, discipline, determination and sacrifice that we put in. The ability to work hard consistently is a gift that we must cultivate in ourselves.

Growing up, I would listen to Indian film music and I really liked it. But once exposed to international music, I wondered why we didn't have musical bands, concerts, private albums, just like there were African bands or European bands. Except for ghazals or qawwali concert recordings on audio cassettes, we did not have the concept of private albums. All of our pop songs were tethered to film. In technical terms, this also meant that our scores were of lower quality, as film had a carrying capacity of 6 KHz while DVD could carry up to 18 KHz. I had a desire to see Indian music on charts internationally, to be heard abroad and to have a life separate from film. Globally, the soundtrack is released separately from the movie. So, I asked why we didn't have separate mixes for the music release and the film. The prevalent answer was that it would be a more time-consuming affair. While most people would have accepted that as rationale enough, I wasn't convinced by this line of reasoning. Western bands at the time would take up to two years to create a great song, but in India, people were doing it in seven hours or so.

While I was not content, I did not complain either. I went ahead and created what I felt needed to be created—high-quality, original scores that younger people could relate to. It indeed took me more time. It took me a week to create what other people could do in a day, and I also put in more effort and discarded more iterations, as I did not want to be restricted by the film's timelines and compromise on the quality of the music. My insistence on quality and excellence also meant taking on less work than others and being less prolific in my output, despite the fact that I had familial responsibilities due to the early passing of my father. But I didn't compromise on quality, and that is what it boils down to—making that extra effort, going that extra mile and never settling for mediocrity.

I do believe that the Divine manifests itself through you, but only when you are sincere in your effort. You won't be a conduit for the Divine while doing something half-heartedly. I am a spiritual man and a man of faith, and I am also a consumer and a lover of music. Hence, my music blends the spiritual or classical with the contemporary or popular. As a believer in the unity of being, I do not accept the silos of genre, language, the classical–contemporary divide, the spiritual–consumerist duality, etc. I strive for both critical acclaim and commercial success. This belief is reflected in my work, making it unique. That is why, when people ask me what the recipe for greatness is, I offer a more mundane answer rather than a philosophically loaded one. When I create music, I think of myself as the consumer. I ask myself what kind of music I want to hear. Is my music to my own liking? Think of it as cooking. If you can't stand your own cooking, how do you expect to serve anyone else? If I can't stand my own music, how can I expect to serve it to others? I serve myself first, then I serve others.

To this, you might say, 'Well, Rahman sahab, your tastes are different than those of the masses.' But I never make the mistake of thinking this way. I think of the masses as discerning experts, as connoisseurs of music, not as people with inferior taste. Now, *that* is what differentiates my music. If you do not respect

your audience and if you think that the public does
not know better, you will keep delivering substandard
products. But you forget that your output defines
you, not your audience. Your work speaks for you;
it represents you. So, when you respect your clientele,
audience or demographic and offer them better
products, better content, better music, better cuisine,
better fashion, better governance, better roads, etc.,
you elevate yourself and improve your own standing.
This is my advice to younger people going into any
field: see yourself as the client, the consumer or the
audience. Begin with, 'I want . . .'—what is it that you
want to consume but find missing? For example, I said
to myself that I wanted to listen to soulful melodies or
something that stood out from the crowd.

So, when I began my partnership with Mani
Ratnam sir, I told him, 'I want this' and 'I want that'—
referring to the musical trends that I observed around
myself and which I felt the youth craved and aspired
for Indian music to reflect. I used to set up equipment
for bands at IIT Madras and found a huge disconnect
between what we were offering and what the youth
wanted. So, I told Mani sir that I want our film music
to be on charts internationally, and I want people
abroad to listen to our music and see what India has
to offer culturally. This was my aim, my visualization,
my manifestation—whatever you want to call it—
and I said to Mani sir that we should do whatever it
takes to get there. Luckily, he understood my vision

and the *Roja* soundtrack (1992) kicked off what was described by the press as a new era of Indian music, even making it to *TIME* magazine's list of 'World's 10 Best Soundtracks of All Time'![1] We worked together on eighteen films until 2023, releasing soundtracks in both Tamil and Hindi, making double the effort and double the impact, bagging well over fifty awards, a dozen nominations and several distinctions. The rest is history.

In product development, UI/UX research evaluates the features of a phone or an app from a user point of view. Similarly, we—musicians—need to think as listeners and ask what features we would like in the music that we listen to. Then, in order to develop those features, if you need to work for two years, you work for two years. If you need to research, you research. For example, in India, industrialists have started asking such questions. We can now find goods and services in the Indian market that one could earlier hope to get only abroad. We are already beginning to manufacture semi-conductor chips domestically. There is tremendous scope in all fields, from horticulture and fashion retail to solar panel manufacturing and mental health services. If every young Indian contributes what is missing in each field, there's no doubt that we can become a developed nation by 2047. I was in Hollywood from 2009 to 2015, but I returned to India in 2015 with the realization that India is the place to be, and there was no use being in the West. At the time, a new India was taking shape, and a new way of doing things was emerging, which I found exciting. My decision to return was also shaped by my desire to give back to my country, which gave me everything, and to the society whose support and admiration propelled me to fame. Through the K.M. Music Conservatory located in Chennai, I hope to nurture young talent and pass on my skills so that we can have many more Rahmans and Mangeshkars to offer the world.

For decades in India, we thought that the West has something that we don't have—something that sets them apart and makes them special—better talent, perhaps. But after years of living, working and collaborating abroad, I realized that, for distinction, what matters most is having a leadership that is unwilling to accept mediocrity and unwilling to compromise on quality. Good leadership entails setting high standards, helping people to realize their true potential, showing them the way, and inspiring them to do better, even if that takes days or months. It involves asking questions about how we do things. For instance, we may ask how others record sound and why we do it a certain way. At times, we may learn from the West, and at times, we may provide our own template for the world to follow, but all of this requires critical observation, paying attention, asking questions about the process and so on.

At times, a problem requires a fresh approach. Keeping at it relentlessly in the same manner won't yield a different result. So, it is okay to take a break and come back with a fresh mind. At times, we simply fail, and that's okay. Failure can be a gift too, because it could be God's way of stopping you from going down a certain path that is not meant for you or is simply wrong for you. It is important to keep our motivation and morale high during these times. That is where faith and spirituality come in. Submitting to a higher power and accepting a greater will can protect us from frustration, agitation and hopelessness. Faith in ourselves and our abilities, combined with the belief that there is a larger plan, can save us from becoming desperate or despondent.

We have a lot to offer the world, but it has to be offered in a format that can add value and be in dialogue with global trends. As a nation, we are finally coming of age, achieving distinction in various fields and coming out at the top in fields like sports, technology, etc. In February, 2024, India won five Grammys—three of them bagged by Ustad Zakir Hussain*, including one for his fusion band Shakti.[2] We are rooted in our civilizational strengths, but in dialogue with the world. In 2020, filmmaker Shekhar Kapur invited me to Dubai and introduced me to Her Excellency Reem Al-Hashimy, who is the minister of state for international cooperation and CEO of Expo

---

*Ustad Zakir Hussain, in February, 2024 became the first Indian to win three Grammy trophies in a single night.

City Dubai. She asked if I could put together an all-female orchestra. I loved the idea, so we began the auditions for it, inviting musicians from all over the Middle East.

For two years, I mentored fifty spectacular women from twenty-three Arab countries, and they performed at various events in the Expo Dubai 2020 (held in 2021–22) using instruments such as the oud, qanun, buzuq and the sitar. Known as the Firdaus Orchestra, it was led by Lebanese conductor Yasmina Sabbah, an exceptionally talented artist. The Firdaus Orchestra took the Arab music scene by storm, and it is something that I'm truly proud of. It didn't disband after Expo Dubai and has now assumed permanence in the shape of 'Firdaus Studio by A.R. Rahman'—a world-class facility located in Al Forsan Zone, Expo City Dubai.

As a young music composer a few decades ago, I lacked exposure to international music; therefore, I aim to provide it to my students right from the start. At the K.M. Music Conservatory School of Music, we bring artists from all over the world to mentor young, raw Indian talent so that they are prepared for the requirements of the global arena and are in conversation with it. We must be proud of ourselves as Indians, but we must not be oblivious to global competition and trends.

As India finds its rightful place in the world, all of us must contribute to it by finding the missing pieces of the puzzle and putting them together. Parents have a huge role to play here in terms of encouraging kids to explore a diversity of careers beyond the traditional few. I must credit my mother for encouraging me to become a composer. I began composing music using my father's instruments at the early age of thirteen, as a result of which I even dropped out of school. Normally, a parent would be alarmed at such a disastrous consequence, but she is a visionary who did not think of musical education or vocational education as any less than formal education. In India, if a child picks up a guitar or an instrument, he or she is discouraged by saying that such hobbies should be pursued after finishing college. But my mother was ahead of her time. Being a composer's wife, she understood and respected the craft, and being a spiritual person, she was able to see my path, my destiny.

Rarely is art or music seen as a career path or as the main vocation, but my mother aced parenting in this regard, inculcating in me a deep respect for work, and ensuring I never had any regrets about leaving formal schooling in favour of my passion. I follow a similar approach with my children, allowing them to find their path wherever it takes them, not imposing my expectations upon them. However, since all of my kids have shown interest in music, it is simply my job as a father to ensure that I guide them as best as possible in their chosen direction. Tomorrow, should they decide to do something different, I will be there for them as a loving parent, and I implore all Indian parents to follow a similar approach with their kids, who are already burdened by homework and societal expectations.

I spent my childhood in the studio, working alongside people who were fifty to sixty years of age while I was thirteen or fourteen. I was barely eighteen when I bought my first computer in December 1984. Technology has always been an integral component of my work. I am lucky that I got a free hand to experiment with my inheritance—my late father's musical equipment—and doing so put me at ease and gave me a comfort with technology that does not always come naturally to people of artistic bent. More recently, we used Artificial Intelligence (AI) to recreate the voices of two deceased singers, demonstrating a fair and ethical use case for AI-generated audio technology. We sought permission from their families and duly remunerated them. Doing so has provided a template for what *should* be done with technology.

We keep complaining about deepfakes, pointing out their ethical concerns and so on. However, whether we like it or not, the technology is already here. So, I thought, why not demonstrate how these technologies *should* be used instead of complaining about misuse? Why not set a precedent for remunerating artists whose voices or images are used to generate content? We have seen the faces of actors being unethically used without permission or consent, and they are fairly helpless in the face of such incidents. However, we have set a precedent for fair and ethical use of such technologies, which can hopefully empower artists to claim remuneration, compensation or damages if someone uses their voice or face without permission. That can be the only deterrent against unethical use. Bad things can only be countered by good things.

I'm not a fan of alarmist views of technology and AI, because they can never replace wisdom, knowledge and experience. Elbert Hubbard famously said, 'One machine can do the work of fifty ordinary men. No machine can do the work of one extraordinary man.' Any writer who has tried out tools like ChatGPT knows that they are nothing more than a better, more improved version of Google, unable to replace even a moderately good writer. We should use such tools to assist us and speed up our work, just as we used search engines.

We can think of such tools as slaves, going by the old adage that technology is a good slave but a bad master. AI assistants can help us shorten the duration of a project. What would take three years earlier can now take three weeks. Problems begin when we allow technology to become a master, as we have to some extent with smartphones and social media. AI has its limitations, which become apparent in the simplest of tasks. If you are a seasoned craftsman or an original thinker, technology will be a mere tool for you. But if you use it as a shortcut, becoming dependent on it, you will be enslaved by it.

At the time of writing (February 2024), we are experimenting with a subaltern AI-based fusion band named Project Secret Mountain, trying to expand the horizons of collaboration and to explore how technology can serve our priorities instead of letting technology define our priorities as we have allowed smartphones and social media to do. As musicians, we do not feel threatened by AI or generative AI, because God has bestowed the power of original thinking only upon humans.

What we need to imbibe, therefore, is leadership thinking, and we need to use this power of original thinking to take initiative and assume responsibility. Someone may build a unique school or centre of learning, someone may write a book, someone may start a hospital, someone may build an artistic monument for India that everyone can take pride in or someone may start a consultancy services company to create jobs and pull people out of poverty—we should think of ways of owning our country and serving it.

As Muslims, what we do defines our community. We should build up our character because it is our image that people associate with our community. When an Indian goes abroad, what he or she does can earn all Indians a good name or a bad one. Similarly, we as Muslims should think of ourselves as ambassadors of our community. People understand our community through our actions and deeds. So, we should try to embody good values.

The Prophet (PBUH) did not merely preach kindness; he embodied it. He didn't just ask us to be compassionate; he *was* compassionate. He didn't simply tell people to be trustworthy; he *was* trustworthy. He was both the walking Hadith and the walking Qur'an. Two billion adherents across the planet do not follow his teachings simply because he preached good values, but because he exemplified them. While it is not possible for us to emulate those values, even attempting to do so will elevate us. We should embody the change that we want to see in our country. We can complain that our country doesn't have *this* or doesn't have *that*, but assuming the responsibility of filling the perceived gaps will not only take our country forward, but us as individuals too. We can complain that our country does not have enough communal harmony, but what stops us from building bridges?

We can become more religious and more tolerant at the same time through inwardness, by finding spirituality and purpose within ourselves and focusing on our own relationship with God and with ourselves. I like the concepts of *tasawwuf* (inwardness) and *ihsan* (excellence) in Islam, and I believe in experience more than learning, both in my work and in my faith. When we truly follow a faith, any faith, the only output can be love and excellence. Faith should not be allowed to divide us. The teachings of a faith are universal—they are meant for everyone, not just the adherents. There are good things in Hinduism, Buddhism and all other faiths. We can derive learnings from the lives of Lord Ram or the Buddha if they resonate with us.

I believe that the time has come for people of faith and spiritually oriented people to prioritize both *deen* (religion) and *dunya* (worldly affairs) to build businesses and institutions that benefit everyone regardless of religious affiliation. People of faith can do amazing things because they believe in something that they can't see, a quality that is required for imaginative tasks such as setting up a business or an institution that will outlast them.

I may be venturing into dangerous territory here, but is it possible that our mosques can also function as community centres as they do in the West? Can they run innovation centres on the side for semi-skilled youth, taking both *deeni* (religious) and *dunyawi* (worldly) learning together? Is it possible that the next breakthrough in sustainable transport or the next IKEA (innovation in furniture) could come from one of these community centres? They could avail of government schemes such as the PM *Vishwakarma* scheme aimed at helping artisans who rely on hand work—many of whom are Pasmanda Muslims.

I'm simply thinking out loud and giving an example of something that is not being done, but there can be many other ideas. We just need to start thinking in new ways as to how we can use the power of faith to strengthen India and showcase the positive side of our faith, religion and community. I would like to compliment Shehla for bringing out this book—it fills a vacuum that existed in contemporary literature about the achievements of living Indian Muslims. I hope that it fills the void, showcasing a positive side of our community and inspiring younger people to work for the nation.

I implore younger Indians to similarly find the missing pieces of the puzzle and contribute to building a developed nation by 2047, a dream that all of us share with our Hon'ble Prime Minister. Indeed, the various contributors to this book have done just that—made original contributions to their respective fields. The year 2047 will mark 100 years of our freedom, and we must ask ourselves whether we are using that freedom to realize our true potential as individuals and as a country. Jai Hind!

The Sky Is No Longer the Limit for India

—Nigar Shaji

- Nigar Shaji works at the ISRO as programme director and is currently responsible for all low-earth orbit (LEO) spacecraft as well as all interplanetary missions, including the famous Chandrayaan-3 mission.
- She is also the project director of ISRO's Aditya L-1 solar exploration mission. She was formerly the associate project director of Resourcesat-2A and prior to that, the division head of telemetry subsystem realization at the U.R. Rao Satellite Centre.
- An electronics and communications engineer, she distinguished herself by developing various modules indigenously at ISRO at a time when India was facing import embargoes.

I was born and raised in a town called Sengottai, in southern Tamil Nadu. I had a happy childhood, and my father, Sheikh Meeran, a mathematics graduate, had a huge influence on me. A mathematics and physics enthusiast, he instilled in me a deep love for both subjects which are the basic ingredients of space science. He chose to focus on agriculture because we belong to an agricultural family, but his outlook was universalist. He laid strong emphasis on girls' education and women's financial independence, often telling me stories of Nobel laureates and other inspiring people.

Among the various life stories, the one that stuck with me the most was that of Madame Marie Curie, who literally dedicated her life to science. She became my role model and I wanted to be a scientist like her. I went to a nearby government school, and excelled in both studies and sports. I was inspired by people who did something new, something adventurous and out-of-the-box. So, I was also inspired by Kiran Bedi, who was the first and only female IPS officer in India while I was growing up.

After I finished schooling at the SRM Government Girls Higher Secondary School in Sengottai, I secured admission to the College of Engineering, Guindy, Chennai, but my parents weren't keen on sending me so far away from home to such a big city just after passing the twelfth class. While they were not orthodox, it was perhaps too daunting a thought to let go of their dear daughter so soon.

So, as destiny would have it, I attended the Government College of Engineering, Tirunelveli, graduating with a BE in electronics and communication (E&C). I had to live in a hostel anyway, but Tirunelveli was closer to home than Chennai. That said, Tirunelveli was no small city either, attracting students from bigger cities, including Chennai.

A major challenge that I faced at college, therefore, was that most of the other students spoke fluent English while I struggled significantly, despite having studied in the English medium. I had knowledge and skills, but I lacked exposure, which made me feel intimidated at first. Where I came from, English had been only a medium of instruction, not a language in which we would converse with our friends, family or even teachers, unlike in big cities where English is often the thinking language. For a year, I worked very hard and caught up on my English skills while also excelling in engineering.

I took special interest in mathematics, radar engineering and communication engineering, which were my favourite subjects. Back then, we didn't have much of a culture of campus placements, so I started looking for a job after my studies. I would be lying if I said that it had been my dream to join ISRO since childhood. However, after my graduation, when I saw an advertisement for a vacancy at ISRO for someone with a background in E&C, I had a feeling of awe and told myself that I must apply. I was selected, and I joined ISRO in 1987.

I was inducted into an amazing work culture, with seniors who were very supportive, giving me an opportunity to learn a lot. I first joined the Satish Dhawan Space Centre in Sriharikota, which is the launch base of ISRO, mostly working on radar technology, as my branch was electronics. After four years, I got married and sought transfer to Bangalore, where I joined the U.R. Rao Satellite Centre (URSC), which is the lead centre for making spacecraft. Initially, I worked on the testing side and was involved in developing various test equipment for testing spacecraft. I spent almost twenty years working on the testing of most of the communications and remote sensing spacecraft. While at ISRO, I also did my ME in E&C engineering from Birla Institute of Technology, Mesra, which was my first experience of attending a private educational institution.

I also worked on the development side of test systems, such as for the testing of the high-resolution remote sensing satellite IRS-1C project during 1995–98. In the early 2000s, I also worked on developing the high-rate data acquisition system for testing the payloads of the Earth-imaging satellite IRS-P5 (also known as Cartosat-1) in-house. At the time, India was facing an embargo on the import of high-tech parts due to dual-use concerns, and the private company tasked with developing the instruments failed to deliver them on time. So, I stepped up and managed to develop them and deliver them in time for the launch.

Due to India's specific historical circumstances, ISRO has had to develop two unique qualities—frugality and indigenous development capabilities—which have become woven into our organizational culture. Following that, I worked on the in-house development of various modules. At URSC, I was the first one to work on digital signal processing techniques. This was the time when field programmable gate arrays (FPGA) were being introduced, and we were transitioning from analogue systems to digital. I then became the head of URSC's telemetry division, contributing to the development of the telemetry subsystems onboard all the ISRO spacecraft. From there, I moved on to the next step in my career ladder, becoming the associate project director for Resourcesat-2A.

After that, I was appointed the project director of the Aditya L-1 solar exploration mission, which was the brainchild of Dr U.R. Rao, former ISRO chairman. Initially, Aditya L-1 was planned as a small LEO spacecraft with a single instrument on board. But drawing confidence from the successes of Chandrayaan-1 (2008) and the Mars Orbiter Mission (Mangalyaan, 2013), he revised the scope of the Aditya mission to L-1 orbit with seven instruments onboard, upgrading it to the status of an observatory, as we now had the experience of two successful interplanetary missions to learn from. I am proud to have brought his vision to fruition as the project director of Aditya after his passing in 2017. The importance of Aditya can be understood in terms of the insight that it can give us into space weather.

You know how we predict the weather on Earth so accurately nowadays? Your phone warns you about imminent rainfall hours in advance so that you can carry a raincoat. All that is possible due to satellite imagery and the processing of vast amounts of data. Similarly, there are solar flares, geomagnetic storms, and coronal mass ejections, phenomena that constitute space weather and are studied by heliophysicists.

Space weather phenomena can sometimes impact space assets, astronauts in space stations, high-frequency radio communications and the electric power grid. Since we do not fully understand the occurrence, frequency, likelihood and impact of these phenomena, we cannot brace ourselves for their effects as yet. That is why Aditya L-1 is an important project. Not only India but the world is looking to it for new insights, data, explanations and predictions.

As programme director, I currently oversee all LEO spacecraft as well as interplanetary missions, including the famous Chandrayaan-3 mission. I am very fortunate to be a part of ISRO, as I have never experienced anything like a glass ceiling. In fact, my sense is that the representation of girls in STEM (science, technology, engineering and mathematics) fields in India is better than that in many western nations, where there is a huge ongoing conversation about the underrepresentation of girls in STEM fields.

However, where we tend to lag behind is women's workforce participation, which requires policy redressal. Various initiatives of the Department of Science & Technology (DST) exist, such as Vigyan Jyoti, GATI, WISE-KIRAN, WIDUSHI, WINGS and CURIE, and women scientists should come forward and take advantage of these.

Women also need to come forward and seek the support of family, society and employers in accommodating their unique needs. If you make yourself strong, knowledgeable, skilled and an indispensable worker, no employer will deny you menstrual leave when needed or refuse to support you when your child is ill. My father used to motivate me by saying: 'If the mountain doesn't come to you, you go to the mountain.'

No one will hand success to us on a platter. We need to be positive, motivated and ready to step up, embrace opportunities and get our hands dirty. The ISRO is India's pride for a reason—it is a meritocratic organization where you are not judged by your identity, status, gender, etc. Your credentials alone determine your place in the organization. Despite high organizational discipline, it is not a hierarchical organization in the negative sense of the word. Anyone can come up with good ideas, insightful arguments and fresh questions.

Space science continues to be an enigma; therefore, no ISRO member walks around with arrogance about his or her knowledge. In fact, our exposure to the world of stars is a humbling experience for the simple reason that we are highly aware of our modest space in the universe. The more knowledge we gain, the more we are astounded by our lack of knowledge, as humans, about God's beautiful empire.

The aim of all space science pursuits is to find life elsewhere or explore the possibility of a second, habitable world somewhere in the galaxy that we can reach in a finite amount of time. That explains the significance of Chandrayaan-1's conclusive proof about the existence of water on the moon's surface. While it does not mean that we can live on the moon as yet, it does mean that the moon can be a potentially viable base camp for further interplanetary missions.

The search for crucial space resources is also an important facet of space science. As fossil fuels run out and we need more alternate sources of energy, this aspect will become crucial in the future. One of the main tasks of Chandrayaan-3's infrared spectrometer was to survey the mineral fingerprint of the lunar surface, and future missions will have this as an important mandate.

We have reason to be proud as Indians, because India is the only country to have successfully placed a satellite in Martian orbit in its first attempt. India has defied all limitations and surpassed all expectations. The Chandrayaan-3, Mangalyaan and Aditya L-1 are the pride of India and the envy of many. With these successful missions, it is clear that the sky is no longer the limit for India. We are looking to soar higher, put our men and women on the moon, set up a space station, land on Mars, develop the commercial aspects of space (including space tourism) and we want to be ahead of everyone else.

However, we need more young Indians to take up the serious pursuit of pure sciences and fundamental research. We also need to place more emphasis on the innovation side. The secret to our shoestring budgets and frugality is local talent and human resource. While we need engineers and technicians, we also need mathematicians, physicists, theoreticians, etc. We hope that programmes such as Chandrayaan, Gaganyaan, Mangalyaan and Aditya L-1 will inspire our best minds to take up fields related to astronomy and outer space exploration. I agreed to contribute to this book because I want to reach out to younger boys and girls, including Muslim girls, and encourage them to take up this path.

When we ask a girl child what she wants to be, she is likely to say something very ambitious. However, as we grow up, we face things like societal stigma, body shaming, discouragement from participating in sports, etc. All this erodes our self-belief and confidence in our own abilities. While this may be true all over the world, it is a little more prevalent among our Muslim community. So, my message to girl children is to have confidence in their abilities and never think of themselves as any lesser than boys.

However, self-belief alone is not enough. It is only the first ingredient of success, and it must be accompanied by hard work and perseverance. My message to parents is to allow girls to study and let them do whatever they want, be it metallurgical engineering or basketball. In all fields, girls are outperforming boys. I want to tell Indian parents, including Muslim parents, to have faith in their girls and let them rise and shine. Their success is India's success.

Campaigns like 'Beti Bachao, Beti Padhao' (save the girl child and educate the girl child) are important for spreading this message in clear and simple terms. It can be said that my father was a visionary, and I can say with certainty that I made him proud, fulfilling his vision and dreams. However, I have also seen my peers and girls my age being married off early and denied the opportunity to study further. Studies and professional life can continue along with family life. Today, we live in a modern society where it is understood that both men and women should participate in child-rearing and share familial responsibilities. We have new provisions like paternal leave alongside maternal leave, signalling a shift in parenting trends.

My children and my husband are not my limitation, they are my strength. They take pride in my achievements, and our family is like a team, where the mother alone is not burdened with household chores. Everyone in the family plays his or her part. I could do something big for my country because my family, including my father, mother, husband and children, believed in me and supported me. As a society, therefore, we need to realize and harness the full potential of women so that India may progress. We cannot progress if any section of society—be it Muslims, women or anyone else—lags behind. So, we must gear up, lean in and take charge of our destiny. Inclusive development is possible only when each one of us contributes their best output to national development.

With the Government of India's increasing focus on defence indigenization, domestic manufacturing of semi-conductor chips, search for critical minerals, etc., it is even more important for us to build domestic capabilities and replicate the ISRO model of excellence by having high-end, local talent. Academic institutions should try to increase private and public sector collaborations so that students have an early orientation towards what is expected of them in our ever-growing economy. It is not necessary for everyone to be an engineer. The National Education Policy 2020 enables students to explore their niche by incorporating interdisciplinarity.

It is not the field we are in that determines our success; it is the way in which we approach our field that makes the difference. I want to make a small differentiation between 'promise' and 'merit'. When we qualify an entrance test or ace a competitive exam, it is only a show of promise. Merit is when we realize that potential and that promise, making the best of our capabilities. Hence, we should not think of competitive exams as the end goal but as a means to achieving our goal and as a platform to showcase our promise. Merit requires being sincere and passionate about your work and staying motivated despite difficulties.

After the failure of Chandrayaan-2, it took us a while to gather our spirits, even though ISRO is a self-motivated organization. In space science, even a small mistake can cost us very dearly. However, the government has been supportive, understanding the criticalities of space missions and allowing us to fail. This is how Indian parents should behave with their children: give them a hug when they fail, and then watch them rise like a phoenix from the ashes, as we did with Chandrayaan-3's globally acclaimed success.

The 'Gen Z'* or as Prime Minister Narendra Modi puts it, 'the *Amrit Peedhi*'[1] thinks outside the box, and it needs to be supported in its innovative ideas. My message to the Gen Z kids, is that you can achieve whatever you want, and you are only limited by the magnitude of your own dreams. That is the moral of

---

* Generation Z or 'Gen Z' refers to digital natives, roughly born between 1995 and 2010. The term broadly corresponds to the term Amrit Peedhi—the generation that will come of age during the next twenty-five years and contribute to India's economic development. This twenty-five-year period is termed by Prime Minister Narendra Modi as India's '*Amrit Kaal*' (blessed phase)—the last quarter of the century since India's independence. Amrit Kaal represents a vision for India to become a developed and prosperous nation by its 100th year of independence.

my story, and that's the story of India's rise. Today, we dream bigger, and it is not foolish to do so. Those who dream may either fail or succeed; but if we do not even dream, failure is assured. If we deploy our demographic strengths optimally, imparting skills to and creating opportunities for the Amrit Peedhi, there is no doubt that we can transform ourselves into a Viksit Bharat by 2047.

On Grand Slams, Girl Power and Building a Better India

—Sania Mirza

- Sania Mirza is one of the most well-known, highest-paid and influential athletes in India. With six Grand Slam titles and the distinction of being India's first and only female World No. 1 in doubles, she has shattered glass ceilings and redefined sporting dreams for young Indians. She runs the Sania Mirza Tennis Academy in Telangana, grooming young talent for excellence in tennis.

- In 2004, she received India's second-highest sporting honour, the Arjuna award. In 2006, she received the prestigious Padma Shri, India's fourth highest civilian honour. In 2015, she received the Major Dhyan Chand Khel Ratna

Award, India's highest sporting honour. In 2016, she received the Padma Bhushan, India's third highest civilian award.

- She was named in *TIME* magazine's 2016 list of the 100 most influential people in the world[1]. A brief list of her achievements:

  - Six Grand Slam titles (three doubles and three mixed doubles)
  - Eight Asian Games medals (two golds, three silvers and three bronze)
  - Four Afro-Asian gold medals.
  - Two Commonwealth Games including a gold (doubles)
  - Former World No. 1 in doubles (2015–2016)
  - 43 WTA Tour titles (1 singles, 42 doubles)
  - Asian Games Gold Medal (mixed doubles)
  - First South Asian woman to reach a WTA tournament final (2005)
  - Pioneered a doubles-focused career path for Indian women's tennis

This chapter is based on a telephonic interview with Sania Mirza.

Shehla Rashid (SR): Please tell us about your early childhood. What inspired you to play tennis? And at what age did you begin?

Sania Mirza (SM): I began playing tennis at the age of six, at a time when taking up tennis as a professional career was unheard of, especially for a young girl from Hyderabad! Except for a few pioneers like Mahesh Bhupathi and Leander Paes, we hadn't heard of professional tennis players from India. So, the biggest challenge was simply to summon the self-belief required to visualize becoming the World No. 1 in tennis and getting others to believe in your dream. This was over thirty years ago, when we didn't have the kind of infrastructure and training that we have today. Half the training involved watching tennis legends such as Steffi Graf on TV and analysing their technique.

SR: What were the biggest challenges that you had to face back then? What were your struggles?

SM: Finding the right trainers was as big a task as finding a half-decent court. There were challenges literally on court and off the court. Our tennis courts used to be made out of cattle dung, and if I wanted to play on a hard court, I had to go to a different state to do that! It is wonderful to hear praises and recognition to the effect that, 'You are the first person to do this and that . . .' but it also means that I had to learn everything the hard way. I had to learn from my own mistakes and forge my own path because there was no one else around who had done what I wanted to do.

SR: You achieved your first big victory at the age of fifteen. How did you handle the fame that came with it? I'm sure it wasn't easy. Who or what was your support system through this journey?

SM: Though I am grateful to God to have had a long and fulfilling career, attaining fame at the age of fifteen isn't easy for anyone, and it wasn't easy for me either. Growing up in front of the whole world and being under constant media gaze as a child can be daunting for anyone. You have to present a put-together image on the outside, but nobody knows your internal struggles, desires and anxieties. It meant that I couldn't do the things that other teenagers could, such as bunking class and going to the movies! At times, I didn't want to do interviews. Instead, I wanted to do mundane things that any sixteen-year-old would want to do, such as going out and having coffee, but things weren't so simple for me anymore.

It also meant that I had to work doubly hard at school compared to the other kids. I would train for five hours daily and study for seven hours a day. However, as soon as people saw my seriousness and commitment, they made adjustments to accommodate me. My school, Nasr Girls High School, Khairatabad, would give me special classes and allow me to leave forty-five minutes early for practice. But my sacrifice paid off, and I don't have any complaints in life, given the *rutba* (status) that God has bestowed upon me.

Thankfully, I have the most supportive parents one could ask for. My parents have been my biggest strength, keeping me anchored through all the challenges that I have faced in my life and career, setting a parenting benchmark so high that I have to work hard to live up to it as a parent myself. It is with their support and my sister Anam's support that I won my first Grand Slam title at the age of seventeen! And it was their love that kept me grounded.

SR: What does it take to be a winner, and what is your advice for young girls who want to be successful like you, whether in sports or in any other field?

SM: It took the coming together of my entire ecosystem to make this possible. Champions aren't made by coincidence; they are made when everything falls into place. My advice to young girls is that you must believe in yourselves and follow your dreams. As cliched as that sounds, I cannot emphasize it enough. There are no right or wrong careers, and there is no dream too big. Whether you want to be a doctor, a fashion designer, a make-up artist or a sportsperson, you will need to be serious about your dream in order for others to believe in you.

Society has a list of dos and don'ts for young girls, and it is difficult to get people to believe in our dreams. But don't let that stop you. Persist in your pursuit of greatness and some day or the other, you will get there.

Not everyone will achieve their dream at seventeen; some will need twenty-three years, others thirty or even forty-five years—it is okay to be a late bloomer in life, as long as you are doing what your heart really wants to do. Our dreams matter, no matter how out-of-the-box they might be. In fact, our dream is all that matters! Once your heart is set on something, you will need to follow it up with commitment, sacrifice, perseverance, self-belief and confidence. Daydreaming alone won't suffice.

SR: What is the most important quality for becoming a champion, in your view?

SM: If you aspire to make your name in the world of sports, then you will need stubbornness because sports are monotonous. There is a lot of repetition, and you will need a stubborn focus to do the same thing again and again. You have to believe that every repetition is making you better. This is something I always emphasize with young learners at my academy, the Sania Mirza Tennis Academy. The main quality needed for success is to believe that you deserve success and that you can be the best. Take honest feedback from people, but don't let anyone convince you that you are not good enough. Yes, you may lack skill or practice, but that simply means that you need to work hard, get skilled and put in enough practice—be it in any field.

SR: Did you visualize yourself as World No. 1? Did you believe that it was possible?

SM: Did I believe that I could be World No. 1? Yes. Did I picture myself as the world champion? Yes. Did I know that it was going to happen? No! We cannot know the future, but we can create it through our self-belief and sincere effort.

SR: Would you say that dreaming of becoming World No. 1 is more plausible today than it was thirty years ago when you started? I mean, today, there are role models like yourself for kids to follow, and our sports infrastructure is also much better. At an event held at the Prime Minister's residence by the Indian Minorities Foundation, former athlete Anju Bobby George expressed this sentiment by saying that she was 'born in the wrong era'. What are your thoughts on it?

SM: The support systems and infrastructure that we have today are much better than what we had thirty years ago, when the only sport that we pursued seriously as a country was cricket. The sports infrastructure in India has undergone a massive transformation that young people today can benefit from. We have much more institutional support for sports and many more sporting role models than we did in my day. It would be fair to say that the successes of players like myself and some others like P.V. Sindhu, Saina Nehwal,

Mary Kom, etc. paved the way for others to dream beyond cricket.

We put India on the international map in various non-cricketing events, bringing recognition to non-cricketing events domestically. That spurred infrastructural development, creating champions in less popular sports such as badminton and hockey. In general, the more champions we have, the more seriously our sporting events will be taken. Someone will have to take the lead and show the way in a particular sporting event in order for it to achieve recognition back home.

Once someone shows that it is possible for India to be No. 1 in XYZ field, the entire country starts believing in it. It was not very long ago that we did not have enough gold medals to our credit in the Olympics, but people like Neeraj Chopra changed that.

SR: The government today is visibly and deliberately focusing on sports. How far do you think this has made these successes possible? One of the contributors to this book, para-swimmer Shams Aalam, said that today, the facilities that are available to para-athletes were not even available to able-bodied athletes until a decade ago. Do you think that's a fair account?

SM: It's fair to say that the government has responded in an agile manner, investing in sports infrastructure wherever we have demonstrated even the slightest amount of promise, recognizing talent and grooming athletes for successes that we didn't even dream of until a few years ago.

The facilities available to athletes today are much better than they were before, even though we still have a long way to go compared to countries like China, Australia, the US, etc. We need to continue on this path and make world-class infrastructure available to young athletes in every sporting event. It will take time, but it will need to be done. India has demonstrated seriousness by making a bid to host the 2036 Olympics, which can energize both athletes and sponsors. We will need private investors to step up and athletes to gear up towards this dream. The government alone can't be expected to do everything. Academies, such as my own, will also need to play their part in making us serious contenders for such events.

SR: You raised an important point. While we have achieved success despite frugality, we are competing with the likes of China and Australia. India also hopes to become a developed nation by 2047. What will it take for us to get there?

SM: In our dream of becoming a developed nation by 2047, sports will have to be given a special place. There is no developed country that doesn't take sports seriously, and the government alone can't change this. Everyone should play a sport in order to live a healthy life, as people in the West do. All schools will need to include sports as a serious part of the curriculum in a big way—there should be formal credits for sports achievements and so on.

We need to become a sporting nation, which means all citizens, not just athletes and sportspersons, must see sports as a way of life and not just something we go outside to do. Sport gives you the mental ability to believe that you will always have another day, as long as you want there to be one. It teaches you how to be humble in victory and resilient in defeat. Being an athlete prepares you for life because you learn how to fight, how to emerge from loss and how to continuously improve yourself. Sportspersons are only as good as their last match; hence, we need to constantly strive to be better until the day we retire. We can apply this to all areas and continuously try to be better human beings, better parents, better mentors, better citizens and so on.

In order to be a developed nation, all of us need to think of ourselves as ambassadors, as representatives of India. Representing our great nation is a dream for everyone—it could mean a Sania Mirza representing India in tennis or it could mean a Shehla Rashid representing India's greatness and diversity through a book such as this one. Once we do well in our respective fields, we bring honour and recognition to our profession. And that recognition will lead all fields to develop, propelling us forward. In the sports arena, we will need better infrastructure, better coaching, more corporate sponsors, more financial support from governing bodies, and so on—a convergence of collective efforts geared towards the singular aim of making India a world leader. If we have progressed so much in the last thirty years, there is no reason why we can't progress more in the next fifteen to twenty years.

SR: At the Sania Mirza Tennis Academy, how are you contributing to the dream of Viksit Bharat? Do you also wish to expand the academy and open more branches across India?

SM: At the Sania Mirza Tennis Academy, we are doing our bit by grooming excellence. Through the Mirza Foundation, we also identify deserving players who need financial and logistical support. We are not looking to expand our academy because we want to maintain the personal touch and the quality of coaching that we can currently offer. We are prioritizing excellence over commercial aims. This is how we believe we are contributing to the dream of Viksit Bharat. Everyone needs to aim for excellence in their own field of expertise in order to contribute to this dream. Our commercial aims are secondary.

SR: Sania, you returned to professional tennis after becoming a mother. What is the message you want to give to women who look up to you?

SM: As women, we have as much to contribute to our nation as men do. I returned to professional tennis after motherhood, and I hoped that my decision would inspire at least some young mothers out there to continue to follow their passion and their dreams. It is important to tell young women that their dreams matter and that motherhood is not the end but the beginning of a journey.

A lot of women make sacrifices when they become mothers, forgetting who they are and killing their dreams. My message to them is that you are both an individual and a human, in addition to being a mother. Loving yourself is as important as loving your child. The life that you have created with your loved ones is as important as the life that you had before marriage and motherhood. Every girl, every young person and every citizen needs to understand that India will only be as good as they are! Realizing our potential is a form of national service, so all of us should do that to play our part in making India a developed nation. I wish we had more time, but that's all I have to say today, Jai Hind!

SR: Thank you for your time, and all the best to you for your future projects.

Hard Work Is Its Own Reward

—Huma Qureshi

- Huma Qureshi is a Bollywood actor, film producer and author. Best known for her iconic role in *Gangs of Wasseypur*, she doesn't shy away from unconventional characters, breathing life into complex women on screen, from the unapologetic Monica Machado in *Monica, O My Darling* to the charismatic Maharani in the web series of the same name.

- In the film *Double XL*, she plays a plus-size fashion designer, Rajshri, who navigates societal expectations and body image pressures while chasing her dreams in the competitive world of fashion. Qureshi portrays Rajshri as a confident and ambitious woman who refuses to be defined by her size. She is vocal about her opinions and unafraid to challenge beauty standards, making her a relatable and inspiring character for women who don't fit the conventional mould.

- Her debut novel, *Zeba: An Accidental Superhero*, is about a sassy, witty, irreverent, relatable young woman who is a misfit and a reluctant symbol of female empowerment. How much of it is autobiographical is food for thought!

This chapter is based on a Zoom interview with Huma Qureshi.

Shehla Rashid (SR): Can you tell me about yourself, your family and what it's like to be a first-generation achiever?

Huma Qureshi (HQ): I am a South Delhi girl. My father is from Delhi and my mother hails from the beautiful Gurez Valley in north Kashmir. It would be wrong to call myself a first-generation achiever, as my father runs a very successful chain of restaurants named Saleem's, which is over fifty years old. We can both be considered first-generation achievers in our respective fields. He was the first in the family to make his mark in the hospitality sector and I am the first one in the Hindi film industry. Since I was academically inclined, my mother wanted me to become a doctor and I enrolled in the science stream after high school. However, I quickly realized that my heart was in the humanities and that I was interested in theatre.

SR: So, when did you make the switch from science to the humanities? And when did you actually take up theatre?

HQ: While in my heart I always knew I wanted to act, it took a lot of courage for me to acknowledge it even to myself, as nobody else in our family was even remotely connected to acting. Often, the biggest step towards success is to summon the courage to dream in the first place. So, I initially toned down my dreams, telling myself that I could direct plays or something like that. I began theatre while studying history at Gargi College, Delhi University, and I started getting calls to audition for films from big production houses in Mumbai while I was still a student, which felt surreal at the time! My role models were Madhuri Dixit, Sridevi, Shah Rukh Khan, etc. To think that I was going to work with the same studios that produced their films was the stuff of dreams. However, when I decided to go to Mumbai and give it a shot, my parents, especially my mother, took a lot of convincing, as my family had no prior exposure to the film industry.

SR: Yeah, that's my biggest question. How did you convince them?

HQ: I told my father in a very emotional conversation that if he didn't let me do this, I would regret it all my life, and he would be the reason. I told him that when I get old and get my first role as a grandmother, I'll blame my family and hold him responsible, at which point he had to concede! He could perhaps relate to my situation better because when he started Saleem's in 1972, he had to face opposition from *his* father, as nobody in our family had ventured into hospitality then. So, he gave me one year and asked me to go and explore my dreams in a classic '*Ja Simran Ja, Ji Le Apni Zindagi**'* moment, but he didn't want me to be an eternal struggler in Bombay either. Being very practical, he said that if I don't succeed within one year, I should come back, join the family business, get married and settle down.

SR: That's interesting. Your father seems to be emotional but also practical at the same time!

HQ: Yeah, he allowed me to succeed, but he also assured me that even if I failed, I would have his supportive embrace waiting for me back home. He also helped convince my mother, for which I'm grateful to him. Trust me, your parents want to be the reason for your success. They don't want to be blamed for your ineptitude in a line of work that they chose for you. So, follow your heart and don't blame your parents—this is the first rule of being an achiever. I've heard people say, 'Oh, I couldn't do this because of my parents.'

---

* Reference to an emotional scene from a Hindi movie where an Indian father allows his daughter to explore Europe on her own.

However, we cannot make our parents our excuse for failure. Once you demonstrate your seriousness, your parents will take your dreams seriously.

SR: What's your advice for younger people who want to act in movies like you?

HQ: See, I must be honest with younger people aspiring to get into movies. It requires immense amounts of dedication, hard work, discipline, physical fitness, focus and immersion. It's not simply about having good looks. Acting is a profession as competitive as any other. I must tell you to work hard, but that's a no-brainer. More importantly, you need to know that the saying, 'Work hard and then life will be easy after success' is a myth. It never gets easy. Sorry to break it to you! The more you succeed, the more challenging assignments you are expected to take up afterwards—that is the way professional life works. And it is that much more exciting. If you take on easier assignments after a challenging one, you won't experience the same amount of fulfilment. So, you can only move forward—and this is true of any profession—because being at the same level means stagnation.

SR: That's a really interesting observation!

HQ: Yeah. See. The human mind is wired in such a way that once we achieve something, we don't see it as something remarkable because the sleepless nights and the blood and sweat that go into it make it seem believable and achievable. For instance, when I get an award, I don't feel that it is something outstanding because the amount of hard work that has gone into it makes me say to myself, 'Of course, it had to happen. Of course, I deserved it, given how hard I worked'. So, what I'm trying to say here is that the awards, recognition, fame, glamour, etc. are not the reward. The hard work itself is the reward, and it can only be topped by even more hard work. It is not the awards and ratings that give you professional satisfaction. Knowing that you worked hard and did your best is what results in satisfaction.

SR: So, what you are saying is that hard work is its own reward?

HQ: Yeah. But sometimes you get more output by putting in relatively less work. Don't let such 'easier successes' give you impostor syndrome, because prior hard work sets us up for greater success in the future, even if we put in lesser work later because we come to embody that effort even if we don't realize it. I believe in the concept of cumulative hard work, which means that even if you do not get immediate reward from your hard work in one area or one assignment, it'll definitely help you somewhere else. All the knowledge, skills and experience that we gain help us refine our future body of work. Inspiration can come from all fields and from any prior assignment, even if you don't consciously realize it.

SR: That's such an interesting concept: 'cumulative hard work'. It makes total sense to me. So, how hard do you have to work in your profession?

HQ: See, it's not a matter of 'having to' work hard. Enjoying the process is a necessary component of success and professional satisfaction. The more you enjoy working hard, the easier it will get for you. You won't worry about getting an award if you derive enjoyment from the process. I enjoy working hard, meeting people and being on film sets for twelve hours a day, and that is what keeps me grounded. I don't see it as something that I need to do just because I am famous. So, I don't see it as a burden. I have no discomfort with fame or glamour, as I know how hard I have worked for it. I love working and I enjoy the process of doing whatever I do. I enjoy reading in between my shots, and I love writing, so the process of writing my debut novel *Zeba* was as fulfilling as being in a film, even if it is not as glamorous. I enjoy the fact that I can now produce films, bring stories and ideas to life and put them on the map.

SR: Right! So, what, according to you, is the most important component of success? Is it hard work, then?

HQ: The most important element for success is confidence. This is the attitude that helped me navigate the early phase of auditions and struggles. I would audition with the mindset, 'You may not know me when I walk in, but you'll remember me after I've left the room.' Self-belief and confidence helped me make my mark in a town that was new to me.

SR: But it couldn't have been that simple. Surely, you must have had your struggles?

HQ: I didn't struggle to get roles. The real challenge was finding roles that brought out my best potential as an actor. That is when I really struggled. I felt the roles being offered to me were far more limited in comparison to what I had to offer to the role. An actor is only as good as the roles that she is offered. My struggle was not one of making rent, as I came from a supportive family. My struggle was of a different kind—a soul-searching of sorts. So, I began working towards creating a space for myself where I could do roles like Maharani and the one in *Double XL*, where I felt I could express myself more meaningfully. First, films choose you. But after that, you work hard to choose the roles that you want to play.

This 'Phase 2' in my career is where I'm starting to feel more myself. The roles that I am now playing allow me to express who I am and what I believe in and stand for. What I stand for and believe in is creating a world of equal opportunity for everyone. I would love to use my platform to draw attention to issues of justice—not as an activist because that is not the path that I chose for myself—but as an artist, through my creative power, as a writer, etc. I can express how I see the world or my interpretation of it.

Through the book that I wrote, the roles that I play or the films that I produce, I can contribute to changing people's worldviews on important issues such as body positivity, strong female characters, and equal opportunity.

SR: Huma, I've asked this of each one of my contributors: did you ever feel discriminated against as a Muslim in the professional arena?

HQ: I have worked in Hindi films as well as in Malayalam and Tamil cinema, and I must say that I have never faced any discrimination as a Muslim. I have always been confident in my abilities, and I haven't allowed anyone to define me as this or that. I don't believe in othering of any kind. When people ask me if Zeba is a role model for Muslim girls, I say that she can be a role model for everyone. Why just Muslims and why only for girls?

We cannot let anyone straitjacket us into a certain identity. I grew up in GK-1 and Kalkaji, identifying more as Punjabi than as anything else because our neighbours were all Punjabi! Just to be clear, I'm not genetically Punjabi, but our culture and our surroundings define how we see ourselves.

We would celebrate all festivals as a community. Be it Eid, Christmas or Janmashtami, our colony would organize skits where kids would dress up and act out a play. In fact, the only time when I would feel a blow to my identity was when I would be made to dress up as and play the part of Lord Krishna, despite my desire to play Radha. While all the girls dressed up as Gopis or as Radha, I would, for some bizarre reason, be asked to play Krishna. I would cry profusely each year, not getting to play Radha! I blame my chubby face and curly hair as a kid for making me the perennial choice for playing Krishna, as a result of which my mother bought a yellow dhoti for me instead of looking for one to rent annually. This was my biggest grouse growing up!

SR: So, what is your message to young Muslim readers, especially those who want to be in any role in the film industry—not necessarily acting, but as directors, lyricists or anything else?

HQ: The Indian film industry has always been an inclusive place, and Muslims have always done well in Bollywood, so I didn't face any big challenges due to my identity. It is a secular place, and nobody gets hired for their identity. We get hired because we are good at our jobs, because we can play a part well or sing a song well. In all fairness, the audience does not see us in religious terms, either. I can only speak for my own field, but India has always offered me equal opportunity as a woman and a Muslim. I have received love, and I want to spread love and positivity all around me while being who I am.

Yes, there have been some negative portrayals such as evil Muslim characters in some movies, but, on balance, there's also *Pathan*, which broke all records, getting a crazy reception all over the country. The people of India embraced and cherished it. Unfortunately, due to some vested interests, people like to put forth an agenda, which furthers othering. This is because people are quicker to pick up negative stories as opposed to positive ones, and the former tend to get circulated widely. Hence, being in the limelight, my job is to speak against othering. We shouldn't let anyone other us, and we shouldn't think of ourselves as others based on our gender, faith or region.

SR: That makes sense. Final question: How will Muslims contribute to the vision of Viksit Bharat 2047—this dream of making India a developed nation by 2047?

HQ: Muslims contribute to the nation and always have, but not in isolation. Our biggest supporters are often our fellow citizens from other faiths. This is the

India I grew up believing in, and this is the India that we should celebrate and continue to cherish.

SR: Thank you so much for your time and insights, Huma! It was lovely chatting with you.

HQ: Likewise! Stay blessed.

So, What's Your Excuse?

—Shams Aalam

- Mohammad Shams Aalam Shaikh is a celebrated Indian para-swimmer. He holds the world record for the longest open-sea swimming by a paraplegic person.
- He received the Best Sportsperson with Disability Award from the President of India on 3 December 2021.
- At the Reykjavik International Games held in January 2024, he bagged six medals, including a gold and two silver medals, becoming the World No. 1 para-swimmer in the men's 100 m butterfly (S5) category and the men's 50 m breaststroke (SB4) category, bringing laurels to India!
- He was awarded the best emerging leader in disability sports and sports diplomacy by the US

Department of State Global Sports Mentoring
Program 2018.

- He has won numerous medals at national and
  international competitions.
- He is a motivational speaker and an advocate
  for accessibility and inclusion.

I was born in a small village in Bihar named Rathaus,
which is in the Madhubani district that borders Nepal.
I grew up alongside three brothers and two sisters who
were all educated in the madrasa. The youngest of six
siblings, I was the only fortunate one to be sent to school.
I too went to the madrasa initially, as is customary
for Muslim children in the village, but I shifted to
Mominpura Municipal Urdu School in Mumbai, where
my family moved afterwards. I was educated in the Urdu
medium until the seventh grade. After this, I attended
the Mohammed Haji Saboo Siddik Junior College and
Technical High School, run by the well-known Anjuman-
I-Islam educational society, until the tenth grade.

Lacking much exposure, I inquired around about
good career options and found out that getting a
diploma was promising, as it ensured job placement.
So, I got a diploma in mechanical engineering from
Mohammed Haji Saboo Siddik Polytechnic itself. I
subsequently earned a degree in mechanical engineering
from Rizvi College* in Bandra, as Saboo Siddik did not
offer a degree in my stream. In the seventh semester of

---

*Rizvi College of Arts, Science and Commerce.

my degree, I started experiencing some problems with my mobility. I had trouble walking all of a sudden, and I couldn't understand what was happening, as I had been an excellent karate player until then. I had been a university-level champion in karate and had participated at state, national and international levels, earning around fifty medals. As a result of the trouble with my mobility, my studies were also affected. So, after the end-of-semester exams of the seventh semester, I had to stay back to retake a test. By the time I took the test, after a gap of about six to seven months, I had to appear in the exam in a wheelchair!

For a karate athlete, such a dramatic change was life-shattering. Earlier that year, in June 2010, I had won a silver medal at the National Championship held in Aurangabad, Maharashtra. The top three performers at the National Championship were to be sent to the National Camp for the selection and training process for the upcoming Asian Games to be held in Guangzhou, China, from 12 to 27 November 2010. However, this dream remained unfulfilled as my illness set in.

I secured a job at Wipro through campus placement, but I was ambivalent about it because it was an IT sector job, whereas I belong to what is known in campus lingo as a 'core' branch* namely, mechanical

---

*It is customary for students from 'core' engineering branches such as civil, mechanical, etc. to get placed in IT companies, as *all* engineering graduates, including IT, computer science, etc. need to undergo elaborate training as 'trainee engineers' before they can actually work on projects.

engineering. Although I had joined a sales company while in college just to make a living, my stint there was soon cut short as the second toe of my left leg started to get tense due to a compression. It became difficult to travel by train, as well as to climb and descend steps.

So, I saw a doctor in Leelavati Hospital, Mumbai, who advised me to get an MRI scan done, which revealed the presence of a tumour in my lower back that was compressing my nervous system. The doctor suggested surgery to remove the tumour, failing which I could end up immobile or even dead. He did warn me that post-operative care would require a minimum of fifteen days' bed rest, after which I should be able to walk. So, I took his advice. I remember explaining to him that my mobility was of utmost importance to me, as I was a karate player with a high chance of participating in the upcoming Asian Games. Representing one's nation in the Asian Games is a dream for any player worth his salt. Therefore, I agreed to the surgery without much ado, so that I could recover from post-operative care well in time for the Games. I even had some money saved up and was ready to spend it on my surgery at any good hospital. Despite the financial viability and time-criticality of the surgery, he suggested that instead of Leelavati, which is an expensive hospital, I undergo the surgery at Asha Parekh Hospital in Santa Cruz, where he undertook his practice as well, besides Leelavati.

The doctor seemed like a nice gentleman who spoke to me very well, thus inspiring confidence in me.

I thought he was being considerate about my financial situation without prompting, so it sounded like sincere advice. Anyone who has undergone surgery will know that you tend to go ahead with a doctor who inspires confidence. I consulted two to three doctors at various government hospitals, and each one of them suggested that surgery was important. So, I decided to go ahead with the only option that lay in front of me, optimistic that it would be a matter of at most a fortnight and that I'd be able to join the National Camp. Once the surgery was over, I went for follow-up visits to the said doctor and he kept saying that I would recover in ten days, fifteen days and such. The biopsy report revealed that the extracted 'tumour' was just normal tissue, not a tumour. By now, I had lost all sensation and strength from the chest downward. I also lost control over my bowels and bladder. As days gave way to months, I became depressed and alarmed, to say the least.

So, I went to a rehabilitation centre in Bombay known as the Paraplegic Foundation. After consulting the doctors there, I got another MRI done, whose result was very shocking to me. The MRI revealed that the tumour was still in place, as before, and it was as if the surgeon had only opened me up and stitched me back, leaving the tumour intact and removing only some soft tissue, which was consistent with the biopsy report that the retrieved mass was just normal tissue. This was shocking to me on so many levels. I had lost time, which was crucial. I had lost money. But most importantly, I had also lost the golden window which is crucial for treatment. I underwent a second surgery during which a benign tumour—3 mm in diameter—was indeed removed from my body, as confirmed by the biopsy report that followed. But recovery was not a smooth road now, as I had lost a crucial three to four months between diagnosis and the *actual* surgery. Nevertheless, I joined physiotherapy and went for regular follow-up visits to the doctors.

Six months elapsed. It was now 2011. We had the Internet, YouTube, etc., and we were wise enough to find out the bitter truth about things on our own. So, I too went online and looked up my condition, only to realize that there is no scientific or medical cure for paraplegia. I had been rendered paraplegic by a botched-up surgery and medical negligence, but what had cost me everything was dishonesty on the part of the surgeon. It is one thing to get the surgery wrong; quite another to hide the truth from the patient. I had every reason to believe myself a victim, to be angry and to turn reclusive and bitter. Indeed, I cried and became sad, and it took time for my new reality to sink in. Apparently, I could only mitigate my condition to an extent through physiotherapy, rehabilitation, etc., but there was no cure, no reversal. So, I chose acceptance.

My mother stayed beside me at the rehabilitation centre and became my full-time caregiver, as I had no bowel control. I would involuntarily defecate or urinate while exercising or on the bed. I once remarked to Ammi that I felt bad about the fact that she had to care for me all over again, as she did during my infancy. I was now twenty-three or twenty-four years old and I felt awkward about it, no doubt. When I asked her how she felt about it, she said, 'No worries, Babu (kiddo); maybe I didn't do enough for you when you were small; I'm happy to do it now.' In that moment, I realized that, in a mother's eyes, a child is always a child. She always prayed for me and asked me to stay strong. She would motivate me by saying that if God had shut one door upon me, He would throw open several others. Indeed, He did! But it is to my mother's credit that I stayed strong then. The financial support from my brothers had waned by then as they had to prioritize their own families, and I started to feel the pinch, badly craving productive engagement. So, I picked myself up and took the remaining tests (eighth semester) to complete my engineering degree and I joined a call centre as a customer care executive.

Meanwhile, the Paraplegic Foundation had an annual sports festival where many people like me participated. It was an eye-opener for me to know that paraplegic people too could participate in sports. At the festival, I participated in swimming, discovering one of the 'other doors' that Ammi promised God would open for me. I had never thought that I would pursue swimming professionally, as it was just a life skill that I had picked up by virtue of being born in a flood-prone village. My native village, Rathaus, was downstream from two rivers that flowed in from Nepal to the west. To the east, there was another river. Beside our home was a pond named Pokhar. Ammi used to tell me that even as a child, I would swim and cross the pond, and that I was surprisingly good at underwater swimming even back then. Now, I had discovered para-swimming as a sport, and it has become my life skill in quite another sense!

When I would go for swimming practice, the supervisors at the pool wouldn't let me enter the pool; it was a novel sight for them to watch a wheelchair user trying to enter the pool! But I soon found a mentor named Rajaram Ghag ji—rendered disabled due to childhood polio—who had crossed the English Channel in 1988, swimming from England to France, completing 32.2 km in twelve hours and forty minutes. He encouraged me, but more importantly, he convinced the pool management to at least let me get into the pool and try to swim. As I swam my first 50 m, I gave them a thumbs up, indicating that I could do it. People think that because you can't move your feet, you can't swim. However, disability is a spectrum, and different para-athletes find different techniques depending on their specific abilities. When I swim, it is my shoulders and my core that propel me forward; hence, I need to do a lot of shoulder-strengthening exercises every day. However, para-swimming is incredibly diverse, and each athlete finds their own unique way to excel in the water.

I started practising consistently, and in 2012, I won a bronze medal in one event and a silver in the other, in my category, at the Maharashtra State Championship in Pune. Then, I bagged another bronze at the National Championship held at IIT Madras, Chennai, in 2012. This set my swimming career in motion, as I found out about various sporting events, such as the Asian Para Games and the Paralympic Games. I continued participating in national championships and in 2014, I struck gold!

Swimming not only gave a fresh start to my athletic career, but it also helped mitigate my condition to some extent. I regained bowel control to a large extent, especially while practicing butterfly stroke movements. One of the biggest challenges as a paraplegic is muscle wasting (muscular atrophy) due to a lack of mobility. Astronauts who go into space, for example, are also at risk for muscular atrophy because they do not exert their muscles against gravity any longer, leading to reduced muscle function. Hence, they must maintain an exercise routine while in space. Swimming is a good exercise to maintain one's muscle mass, generally for everyone, but especially for paraplegic people. While my main stroke is the breaststroke, I use all four styles: freestyle swimming, backstroke, breaststroke and butterfly stroke. There is an event known as the 200-metre individual medley, which requires a combination of all four styles. I finished tenth in the world in the individual medley event at the World Championship held in Portugal in 2022.

In 2013, I took part in an open-sea swimming competition and successfully swam 2 km in Raigad. In 2014, I swam 6 km in the open sea in Mumbai within one hour and forty minutes—a feat that made it to the *Limca Book of Records*. In 2017, I broke my own record and completed 8 km of open-sea swimming spanning the Sinquerim–Candolim–Baga stretch in Goa in four hours and four minutes, becoming the world record holder for a paraplegic person completing the longest distance of open-sea swimming. While Rajaram Ghag ji, who was disabled due to polio, had completed a much bigger feat in his category, mine was the first such achievement for a paraplegic. Para-swimming has a classification system that groups athletes based on the type and extent of their disability. This helps ensure fair competition by matching swimmers with similar functional abilities at the national level, even though at the international level there is still scope for refining the categories. I continue to hold the world record for open-sea swimming in the paraplegic category at the time of writing this (January 2024).

In 2015, Sathyabama University, Chennai, offered me a full scholarship for an MBA programme. Though I was working with IBM at this point, I chose to take a career break and get higher education, as I knew fully well the value of learning and knowledge. Our faith and our Holy Qur'an also emphasize the importance of education. So, I completed my MBA in HR and operations. During campus placement, I was offered a job in a bank in Bandra, and I preferred it because it was closer to my home. But I was in for another rude shock when, after finishing my final semester in 2017, I was told by the bank that I was no longer eligible for the job, as 'the job requirements had changed'. The bank rescinded its offer, and I was at a loss to understand why. Their VP had already had three rounds of meetings with me; I had passed the aptitude tests, qualified for the technical rounds and so on. Anyone would feel disappointed at such an experience. However, I clung on to my mother's words about God opening other doors.

Then something interesting happened. In 2018, I got a chance to participate in the Asian Games—a chance that I had lost in 2010 due to my illness. It was as if the clock had turned back! My dream of representing my country came true when I participated in the Asian Para Games, which took place in Indonesia. But just when I thought that fate had shone upon me, there was another twist in my eventful story. The day I received my selection letter, my mother had a fall and suffered a cervical injury. I offered to stay back and take care of her, but she insisted I go. As always, she put me first; she knew what it meant for me to have a chance to make my country, my *mulk* proud, as she put it. Her thoughtfulness motivated me to pursue my dream.

I kept in touch with my mother over WhatsApp calls during this time. But I could not secure a medal, as I finished fourth. On my way back, during the transit at Kuala Lumpur, my brother called to inform me that Ammi had passed away! I am grateful that I made it in time to bid my mother farewell, attend her last rites and see her face one last time. People often wonder how I managed to stay positive in the face of such devastating personal tragedies. The simple answer is that I did not have a choice! I had no other option but to persevere, work hard, struggle and lift myself up because I couldn't afford to be at anyone's mercy. In my situation, it was either persist or die— like swimming in the open sea!

However, by 2019, I had really started to crave the need for a stable job, marriage and companionship. After Ammi's passing, I wanted a family of my own, a lifelong partner and someone to come home to. But starting a family first requires professional stability. During the holy month of Ramazan, I prayed to Allah day and night to help me out, and it is as if my prayers were answered! I had gone to speak at Hella, a company in Pune. One of the directors of the company sat down with me to discuss a project that sought to provide customized wheelchairs to people with mobility disabilities. I was invited to lead the project under the CSR division of the company, the Bal Swavlamban Trust. I continue to lead the project, under which we have created India's first Active-X wheelchair that is customizable, lightweight, foldable and affordable.[1]

Such wheelchairs aren't easily available in India, and they need to be imported at a cost of Rs 3–4 lakh. The

Bal Swavlamban Trust aims to provide it to individuals who need it, against a voluntary contribution that can be waived off if needed. The contributions would be used towards enabling competitive and commercial production of these wheelchairs in the long term. This project was not merely a source of productive engagement but also the culmination of my educational degrees—mechanical engineering and MBA! I felt that life had come full circle and I found purpose. I also realized that while everything else—money, fame and even physical ability—can be taken away from you, education and skills are things that nobody can take away from you! I have been through hard times—times when I even had to borrow money from people. And, indeed, you must have seen people with disabilities begging for alms outside mosques or temples. Hence, for youth in general and for persons with disabilities in particular, I cannot over-emphasize the need for education and skill development.

People with disabilities (PWD) are often ignored when it comes to education or capacity building because the entire discourse around work is ableist by its very nature. Hence, the imagery stuck in our heads when it comes to PWD is that of a beggar! In fact, I have faced such funny incidents, too. I was once crossing the road in Bombay, but I had to stop and wait for the pedestrian signal when a kind lady disembarking from an autorickshaw offered me some loose change without prompting, after paying the auto driver. She probably realized what a faux pas she had committed because I was taking my phone out of my pocket at the same time. I'm not trying to blame society, but there certainly needs to be more awareness around disability issues. I'm trying my best to change that perception. I am lucky to have found my soulmate Saba, and we got married on 27 January 2023. She is able-bodied, and she stood up for our love. However, it is generally felt that PWDs do not need marriage, intimacy or partnership. Love is higher up in the 'hierarchy of needs', whereas disabled people generally struggle to get even their basic needs met. I believe that if people with disabilities are given the opportunity and structure to realize their full potential and participate in the economy, the fulfilment of their familial needs will follow.

While the population percentage of PWD is generally taken to be 2 per cent in India, a World Bank report suggests that the actual figures may be around 5-8 per cent.[2] As per United Nations estimates, 1.3 billion people on the planet experience significant disability, representing 16 per cent of the population[3]. These statistics render untenable the argument that it is inconvenient to make accommodations for a minority, and call for greater visibility for PWD in policymaking. These one billion plus people around the world participate in the economy, pay direct and indirect taxes, and contribute to society in innumerable ways. We are not the exceptional case that can be safely ignored.

'WeThe15', a global campaign for the human rights of PWD led by the International Paralympic Committee and International Disability Alliance calls for greater inclusion and visibility for PWDs[4]. We are not an aberration but a very significant part of the population. The social model of disability requires that the onus of accommodating PWDs be on society. If due accommodations are made, we can contribute on par with or even better than everyone else. Think of Stephen Hawking for instance.

I hate to be political, and anyone who knows me knows very well that I have never had anything to do with politics. But I have seen a visible shift in approach towards PWDs in the past few years, especially after 2018. It is to Prime Minister Narendra Modi's credit that he has used his voice and popularity to raise more awareness, and this reflects in the attitude of various ministries—especially the Ministry of Youth Affairs and Sports—and institutions of the country that have started promoting para-sports at par with sporting events for non-disabled persons. The first-ever Khelo India Para Games held from 10 to 17 December 2023 is a game changer as far as equality of opportunity is concerned, being the first of its kind event in India. When the National Games 2022 meet was held in Gujarat, I put out a video appealing to the PM to hold a National Games meet for para-sports events too. And today, it is a reality.

The facilities for para-sports have been brought to par with those for the non-disabled. The achievements of para-athletes such as Sheetal Devi and Insha Bashir are now highlighted at par with, if not above, those of able-bodied sportspersons. This helps us battle negative perceptions, presenting a more accurate picture of the *abilities* of people with disabilities! I have peers and colleagues who have received phone calls personally from the PM after sporting achievements as well as after disappointments. I couldn't possibly explain how it boosts the morale of a sportsperson when the guardian of the nation personally speaks to us or tweets about us. It is not a mere formality; it shows the importance of para-sports in his mind.

Indeed, the central government has walked the talk— today, para-sporting events receive the same treatment as sporting events for able-bodied sportspersons. Better hotels, better training facilities and better conveyance are now available to us too. I am currently training at the National Centre for Excellence in Gandhinagar, Gujarat, which is a state-of-the-art facility for para-sports where all the facilities are accessible. No one who trains here fails! Indeed, we have fetched more medals than our able-bodied peers.[5] This has also gone a long way in ensuring that para-sports get their due share of recognition. When we were going to China for the Asian Para Games in 2022, both Anurag Thakur (then Union minister of Sports and Youth Affairs) and Union cabinet minister Hardeep Singh Puri had come to see us off.

These things go a long way in changing the narrative so that no other paraplegic person in a wheelchair is offered unsolicited alms! State governments are also slowly catching up, and I am hopeful for a better tomorrow. I have been offered a job by the Bihar government, which is a welcome step. I'm trying my best, through my voice and presence, to change the narrative. I have spoken at various forums about the issues concerning PWDs. Sharing my story through this book is also an attempt to raise awareness. Through this book, I wish to appeal to the government to waive off Goods and Services Tax (GST) on wheelchairs and other assistive devices, so that we may participate fully in the economy.

I also want to reach out to parents of children with disabilities and urge them not to write off their children. Be it a physical disability or a psychological issue such as neurodivergence, etc., we are no less than anyone else. With advancements in science, things are getting better. AI has made navigating interfaces easier and more accessible than ever before. Self-driving cars hold the promise of enabling better mobility for us, while advances in natural language processing (NLP) ensure that people with visual disabilities might soon operate digital interfaces and access all services on par with sighted people. The universe of what people with disabilities can achieve is only expanding day by day, I want to tell them.

However, and I cannot stress this enough, education is the key to achieving our potential—be it for able-bodied persons, PWDs, Muslim girls—anyone. The world is a harsh place, and nobody owes us anything. Justice, rights, equality and access won't be handed over to us on a platter. In fact, life is as unfair as it gets. However, I cannot say it better than Ammi—if one door closes, another will open up. I have always taken adversity as an *agni pariksha* (trial by fire). Think of each setback, failure and disappointment as a trial.

Success is not permanent, and failure is not final. We need to keep improving, upskilling, practising our craft and, most importantly, staying positive. Even today, I practise swimming for at least four hours a day. Combined with physical training and rehabilitative training, we end up training eight to nine hours daily. A seasoned athlete needs to practise just as much as a novice. We can never afford to sit on our laurels. If I can do it, what's your excuse?

I help paraplegics as a peer mentor, educating them on how to manage their bowel activity and urinary system or care for their skin, as constant pressure from sitting or lying down continuously can cause skin rashes or even, God forbid, pressure ulcers if we aren't careful. I raise awareness and help people receive the right counselling and interventions at the right time. Social media has helped me get my message out. It also helped me realize that I'm not alone and that many people all over the world with my condition are well-to-do; not all of them are poor or helpless. This also helped me aspire for a better life.

A Kashmiri gentleman named Yousuf Bhai, whose wife was also in a similar situation, worked at the Paraplegic Foundation rehabilitation centre, which I joined after my surgery. He was an important source of early guidance and support for me. He was very knowledgeable and had been working with paraplegics for ten years when I first met him. Yousuf Bhai continues to support paraplegics even today. Because of him, I understood the importance of providing peer mentorship to others. I held various swimming camps in Mumbai and other places. I started the Para Sports Association, Mumbai, and got it registered officially under the Societies Act, as there was no structured body for para-sports at the state or district levels. The association gave a platform to numerous sportspersons, and I naturally assumed a leadership position.

I am grateful that I have had a chance to live not one but two lives—first as an able-bodied person and second as a PWD. Not once during my journey have I been typecast as a Muslim. In fact, I must say, I have been invited to speak only by secular institutions so far. In the past three to four years, I have been invited by fifty to sixty IITs and IIMs, but I find it strange that the Muslim institutes—even those of which I am an alumnus—have never invited me for a motivational talk. They are probably not even aware that I studied there. This also goes to show the lack of awareness within our own community, as well as the lack of diversity among those who are considered role models for Muslims.

I hope that this book succeeds in showcasing the diversity of our achievements. I am the first para-sportsperson from Bihar to have ever received the President's Award for Best Sportsperson in 2020. Yet, there are more people in metro cities who know me than in Bihar. This may also have something to do with the fact that my story is highlighted more in the English media and less in the vernacular media. I hope this book goes a long way in highlighting diverse role models and showcasing different career paths that are available to children from the Muslim community.

Going the Last Mile

—Dr Jamal A. Khan

- Prof. (Dr) Jamal A. Khan is a renowned immunologist and the founder of Denvax, a treatment protocol that can go the 'last mile' in cancer treatment, equipping the patient's immune system to fight cancer and avoid relapse.

- He is a pioneer in the field of dendritic cell-based cancer immunotherapy in India, having treated thousands of patients with this innovative treatment protocol, Denvax. His contributions have revolutionized cancer treatment and offered hope to countless patients seeking effective treatment. He has performed dendritic cell therapy on over 10,000 patients and counting—the highest in the world for a single practitioner.

- He is also a public health educator, with a viewership of millions on YouTube, Facebook and Instagram.
- He runs the Amim Cancer Trust for patients who cannot afford treatment, named after his grandmother whom he lost to cancer.

I was born and brought up in Rampur, in western Uttar Pradesh (UP), which is famous for its royal cuisine and its connection to Mirza Ghalib, who served as a teacher to Nawab Yusef Ali Khan of Rampur. For those unfamiliar with Rampur, it is a city near Moradabad, which used to be a princely state in British India. My great-grandfather served in the Royal Army and was also a freedom fighter. Rampur has five legislative assembly constituencies. In 1952, after the first elections in independent India, my grandfather became the first elected representative of the Rampur (rural) assembly seat. He was elected thrice as an MLA and passed away during his third term in 1963.

My father was married in 1964, and I was born in 1966. Since I never met my grandfather, his memories were handed down to me by my grandmother, Amim bi, who was widowed at a very young age. She was devoted to us, never letting her children feel the absence of their beloved father. She wanted her sons around, so my father came back from the UK after my grandfather's demise, got married in Rampur and settled down. *Daadi* (grandma) was very close to me, as

I was born just two years after she was widowed. I was fortunate to have a monopoly on her unconditional love, which informs my work even today.

My father was a devout Muslim as well as a well-educated person, modern in his outlook, and never conflicted between faith and modernity. He had been exposed to ideas of humanism, rationality, secularism and modernity in the UK, and his worldview reflected the same. So, I would begin by acknowledging my privilege: coming from an educated family with a progressive outlook shaped my goals and aspirations. Yet, I'm not oblivious to hardship and the travails of life.

Following the land reforms, we went from being landlords to evacuees, and I saw my father struggling financially. He was an advocate but couldn't earn much, as he practised at the district court. Practising at a high court would have required him to relocate, but he didn't want to be away from Daadi and us. His struggles weren't merely financial but also existential: lawyering required manipulation, and that made him uneasy. This instilled in me the strong belief that one should follow his or her calling and do only what one's heart permits. My wife and I have worked hard to ensure that our children have the choice to follow *their* hearts.

Though I studied till the tenth grade at the St. Mary's co-ed convent school in Rampur, which was the best school in town, I was an average student, not a topper.

I was introverted, shy, fearful of my teachers and not very happy with the disciplinary preoccupations of the school management. When I was in the seventh grade, my daadi, Amim bi, was diagnosed with breast cancer and she passed away just before my tenth grade board examination. I witnessed her suffering for three long years, while my father went broke trying to get her treated. He sold whatever was left of our ancestral property for her treatment.

We used to take daadi to Government Medical College (GMC), Lucknow, for chemotherapy, which was a very harsh treatment. On one occasion, she hid in a nearby *dargah* (shrine) in order to avoid chemotherapy. Watching her deteriorate while I was helpless turned out to be my strongest formative experience, shaping my lifelong passion, my calling, my desire to cure patients at an affordable cost and my spirit of service. My whole life story is about the desire to make a difference to cancer treatment and to the lives of cancer patients and their kin. Worldwide, cancer is the leading cause of medical bankruptcy. So, when I was invited to contribute a chapter to this book, I accepted it because of the opportunity to reach more people with vital information about treatment protocols that patients and their kin deserve to know about. My philanthropic initiative, the Amim Cancer Trust, honours her memory.

My mother had attended AMU, but my father never wanted me to study at a minority institution.

He wanted me to attend a secular institution that was more representative of our country's social make-up. So, I briefly attended the Colvin Taluqdars' College in Lucknow, which was founded by a British civil servant named Sir Auckland Colvin in the late nineteenth century. It was a reputed college. However, as destiny would have it, there was a long strike at Colvin College, and the resulting uncertainty made me panic, leading me to explore other options. I wanted to study medicine, but the admissions season was already over. At this point, only AMU offered late admissions, so I joined AMU's reputed faculty of medicine. Here, I did my MBBS, followed by my MD in microbiology, with a focus on tumour immunology. During my MD, I was appointed a lecturer at the Aligarh Medical College, where I met the woman who would go on to become my wife, lifelong research partner and collaborator in my mission, Dr Sharmin Yaqin.

It was during my MD that my interest in academics peaked, and I really excelled in my studies; until then, I had been a mediocre student. Hence, I am a huge advocate of super-specialization, talent identification and helping students find their niche. Microbiology students had access to an 'animal house', where we performed experiments on mice, rabbits, etc. As a junior lecturer, I was in charge of the animal house, giving me the requisite space to develop and adequately test the treatment protocol that we practise today. As Aligarh Medical College is one of the most reputed institutions worldwide for medical education, I also got a chance to network with researchers from across the world who would write me letters and send me their publications. We are talking about the time around 1990 when email wasn't around.

One of the researchers I used to correspond with, Dr Sk Md Fazle Akbar from Bangladesh, was a disciple of Ralph M. Steinman, professor of immunology at Rockefeller University, New York, who, in 1973, had discovered and named a new cell type that he called the 'dendritic cell'. He demonstrated that dendritic cells can activate T-cells, a cell type that has a key role in adaptive immunity, helping the body develop an immunologic memory against many different substances. His contribution and, by implication, the importance of dendritic cell immunotherapy were recognized only in 2011, when he received the Nobel Prize in medicine for his discovery of the dendritic cell and its role in adaptive immunity. What the Nobel Committee didn't know is that Steinman had himself died of cancer three days before the Committee finalized his name as the winner!

Cancer is an ominous word, one that people readily associate with death. However, unlike infections, cancer is not an external thing. It is a by-product or an extension of the very life process that turns a weightless embryo into a baby weighing 3 kilos at birth, following trillions of cell divisions within nine months. Cells undergo growth, multiplication, specialization, unite to form tissues and organs, and eventually undergo ageing and natural death—a cycle we are all familiar with. What may be less apparent is the fact that abnormal growth, represented by cancer cells, regularly occurs within our bodies and is consistently identified and combated by our immune system. To clarify, the process of cancer cell formation is inherent in every individual. The bloodstream operates as a vigilant surveillance system, traversing the body to detect and counteract any anomalous cell growth. White blood cells (WBCs) constitute the body's natural defence mechanism, scavenging dead or impaired cells, foreign objects, pathogens, etc.

The development of cancer only occurs if, due to an unfortunate twist of fate, a person's WBCs fail to recognize cancer cells as abnormal. More precisely, the body discriminates between 'self' and 'non-self' imprints (rather than normal and abnormal). At times, our body can reject a 'normal' organ donation or a blood infusion because it doesn't recognize this imprint as 'self'. At that time, the patient requires immunosuppressants to calm down the immune response, much like how a pet needs calming when meeting a new family member. For cancer growth to go unchecked, one must have terrible luck, in that one's immune system treats the abnormal growth as 'self' and not as 'other'.

Our immune response can be broadly classified into two types: innate and adaptive (or acquired). The innate immune system is the body's first line of defence and is present from birth. It provides a rapid, *generic* response to a wide range of pathogens without prior exposure to them. It includes physical barriers (like the skin), chemical barriers (such as stomach acid) and various cells (like phagocytes) that engulf and destroy foreign invaders. The adaptive immune system is more *specific* and takes time to develop. It 'learns' to recognize and remember specific pathogens, providing a targeted and tailored response upon subsequent exposure. Key components of the adaptive immune system include B-cells, which produce antibodies, and T-cells, which directly attack infected cells. Vaccination works by training the B-cells and T-cells to recognize patterns (antigens). These cells work together to create immunological memory. The adaptive immune system takes longer to respond initially, but its ability to create immunological memory allows for a faster and more effective response upon re-exposure to the same pathogen. We are more or less familiar with the role of adaptive immunity against infections and foreign objects, but far less familiar with its role in fighting cancer.

Dendritic cells, which are also a type of immune cell, play a crucial role in alerting the immune system to the presence of foreign invaders, including cancer cells. Dendritic cells form the bridge between the innate and adaptive immune systems. They are part of the innate immune response as they can recognize and engulf pathogens, but they also play a key role in activating the adaptive immune response by presenting antigens (the signature of a foreign or abnormal object) to T-cells. In dendritic cell therapy, scientists collect a patient's own dendritic cells and expose them to a small sample of the patient's cancer cells. This process 'teaches' the dendritic cells to recognize the specific characteristics of the cancer cells. Once the dendritic cells are educated, they are reintroduced into the patient's body. Now, these 'trained' dendritic cells stimulate the immune system to recognize and attack the cancer cells more effectively. Essentially, dendritic cell immunotherapy enhances the body's natural defences by boosting the immune response against cancer, offering a promising avenue in the quest for more effective cancer treatments.

A famous cancer specialist was once asked what *really* caused cancer. He gave an answer that is quite controversial: 'luck', he replied. Luck, an unscientific word, is not kosher for a scientist to utter, yet he stuck to his words. While environmental factors, lifestyle choices and genetic predisposition play a part, there's a huge probabilistic element involved that we cannot explain *as yet*. Even genetic mutation is a routine process. But only specific types of genetic mutations produce cancerous cells that are capable of replicating themselves, leading to 'abnormal growth'. It requires that unfortunate stroke of luck, combined with the additional bad luck of the abnormal growth going undetected by the innate immune system, for one to develop cancer. So, cancer occurs when one's luck is doubly unfavourable!

Even after a tumour is removed or eliminated through radiotherapy or chemotherapy, there is no guarantee that the cancer won't return. There's also no guarantee that, if the cancer returns, the body will be able to fight it. Two patients at the same level of disease advancement receiving the same treatment may have a different long-term response: one may develop recurrence, another might not. Chemotherapy bombards the immune system, giving it a second chance to reorganize itself, but this doesn't necessarily happen successfully in every patient. Additionally, we have no way of knowing whether this has happened at all, and it is only through routine follow-up scans that we find out whether relapse has happened or whether the immune system has managed to gear up.

During this 'wait and watch' phase, we can either do nothing or administer dendritic cell therapy. Through our treatment protocol, we increase the odds of preventing relapse, thereby improving the chances of survival for early-stage patients and the quality of life for advanced stage patients. When administered alongside conventional oncological treatments (such as chemotherapy, radiotherapy or surgery) or even subsequently, dendritic cell immunotherapy can form the 'last mile' in cancer treatment, equipping the body to prevent relapse or recurrence by reducing the role of luck and increasing the probability that WBCs will recognize cancer recurrence, if any, and fight it, improving chances of survival from anywhere between eighteen months and twenty years!

Some patients require suppression of the immune system rather than a boost; hence, at Denvax clinics, what we offer is 'customized' dendritic cell therapy. We don't offer a replacement for conventional oncological treatment. Our treatment protocol must be administered in conjunction with chemotherapy or other therapies. At times, we 'sandwich' it between chemotherapy cycles. We culture the patient's WBCs in a lab and expose them to the patient's own cancer cell pattern (antigen), training their dendritic cells to recognize that pattern—somewhat like a vaccination, hence the name Den'vax'. Naturally, this requires cooperation between the oncologist and us, as the antigen extraction is a crucial step.

At the time that Dr SMF Akbar was corresponding with me on the subject in the early 1990s, he had moved to Japan and had started teaching at Ehime University there. He gave me the courage to start clinical trials, taking the treatment protocol from the lab to the bedside. However, I did not get permission to start the treatment at AMU because dendritic cell research was a niche area that not enough people knew about. Had AMU permitted the clinical trials, it could have brought the university further recognition and laurels, but universities in India often discourage innovation, fearing litigation, liability, etc. While I was at AMU, I carried out a lot of experiments and sent my findings and publications to the National Cancer Institute (NCI) in the US. I was invited to the NCI, where I spent six months. However, I returned to India and my family, and started Denvax, our own clinic, in 2004.

My wife Sharmin and I pioneered the use of dendritic cell therapy in India, helping patients from every district and many places abroad. Her support was crucial, as we had two kids to support at the time. But she shared my worldview, insight and expertise, so both of us resigned from our respective departments at AMU and started our venture in Noida, a city in UP, bordering Delhi, that is part of the National Capital Region (NCR). She is a biochemist, and I am a microbiologist. I used to culture WBCs while she did the antigen extraction from cancer cells. It is a marriage of two complementary souls and complementary expertise. As our work grew and we became well-established and mainstreamed over the years by God's grace, we moved our humble clinic in Noida to Vasant Vihar, an upscale locality in South Delhi where our main clinic and nursing home are situated.

In those days, permission for a new treatment protocol required submitting your data to ICMR (Indian Council of Medical Research). So, we sent in our data and ICMR permitted us to begin trials. By the grace of God, we have performed the highest number of dendritic cell therapies in the world, and I cannot begin to explain the satisfaction that it brings us. Having administered over 10,000 therapies and counting, we have a cure or survival rate of 30 per cent. When administered at the right time—that is, in conjunction with conventional treatment—the survival rate goes up to 90 per cent, irrespective of the stage of advancement of the disease or the age of the patient. We have patients as young as three and as old as eighty-four. Many of them have forgotten that they ever had the disease and have gone on to live full lives. One of our patients is now 104 years old.

All patients and their kin deserve to know this because, despite helping a record number of patients worldwide, we have been able to touch the lives of only 10,000 patients in twenty years, whereas every year around a million new patients are added to the pool in India alone, with an annual mortality rate of nine lakh![1] Very few have a survival rate of five years or more. The number of survivors should go up, and there should be many more 'Jamal Khans' performing the therapy. Even though dendritic cell therapy is well-published and recognized within the mainstream scientific world, we need to raise awareness among oncologists who can, in turn, inform their patients. Tumour immunology is taught to every medical student, and our method is not an outlier. The only reason for low awareness about it in India is that it has originated from an individual and not within an institution.

We could have waited for several years to go around the bureaucratic red tape at AMU, but that would have meant denial of an available life-saving process to Indian patients. While we have in-house medical oncologists, radiation oncologists, physicians, intensivists and general practitioners, we do not have radiation and surgery facilities. We do, however, have a thirty-bed nursing home approved by the government where we provide cashless treatment facilities for GIPSA (General Insurance Public Sector Association) insurance holders. Our patients have also successfully claimed CGHS (Central Government Health Scheme) insurance, implying greater recognition for our method. However, as I said, we are a drop in the ocean, and more people need to take it up. Government can promote our treatment protocol as it is an innovative therapy that plays its humble part in making India a hub for medical tourism and contributing to the GDP.

A Message for My Fellow Indian Muslims

Among those who initially believed in me, a significant majority were my Hindu brothers and sisters, some of whom I must mention. My microbiology teacher at AMU, the late Prof. Ashok Bal, was my mentor and the first to believe in me. I am grateful to him for rewarding my curiosity and not discouraging it. Once I started in Noida, I was introduced to the Union of Microbiologists there. Among them, Dr Mithilesh

Chandra really encouraged me to start the treatment protocol. A senior pathologist, she has also served as the deputy director of the ICMR-National Institute of Pathology at Safdarjung Hospital, New Delhi.

In order to set up my clinic, I needed finances. The bank manager at Union Bank, Noida, Mr Gupta, offered to help me without even asking, when he saw my bank balance. Getting a loan of Rs 5 lakh at the time was very difficult for an early career researcher. In today's terms, it is around Rs 50 lakh. However, he gave me an overdraft limit of Rs 5 lakh, which helped me stand on my own two feet and do something positive for society. Cancer treatment is something that the entire society is a stakeholder in; such things are above faith and identity.

At this point, my daughter was four years old, and my son was in kindergarten. I needed to get them admitted to a school in Noida, which again required a lot of money. However, I explained my circumstances to the school administration, and they allowed me to pay the admission fee in installments. Without these little negotiations that make our nation what it is, a young Muslim couple with no institutional backing, no finances and two kids would not have made it to where we are today. This is when I realized that religion doesn't matter.

For my next challenge, I didn't have the advertising budget needed for such an enterprise. Across the road from my residence was Dr Mahesh Sharma's Kailash

Hospital. He was of the opinion that my treatment protocol should be popularized and introduced me to his PRO, Mr Joshi, who simply organized a press conference for me, giving huge visibility to my work across every nook and corner of UP. The next day, the *Dainik Jagran* newspaper carried a picture of me and my wife performing the treatment[2]. My father saw the picture and even offered to liquidate family assets to support our research.

Upon seeing the news, the medical superintendent of Banaras Hindu University (BHU) Medical College Hospital, Dr Saroj Chooramani Gopal (now president of the National Academy of Medical Sciences) called me up to understand my method. When I asked her why she was interested in my treatment, she revealed that her *bhabhi* (sister-in-law) was suffering from gall bladder cancer. She had been operated upon and was given four to six months by the doctors, depending on whether chemotherapy was administered or not.

Dr Chooramani, after understanding my method, placed her faith in me and brought her bhabhi to me on the seventh day of my practice, being the MS at BHU Medical College herself! We administered dendritic cell therapy to her alongside chemotherapy, and she remained disease-free for two years. Two years later, I ran into her at a wedding, and I noticed her looking frail, so I asked her to come in for a follow-up. Unfortunately, she had developed metastasis. She eventually survived for two and a half years after her treatment with me began. Treating her bhabhi lent credibility to our method, as Dr Chooramani is a renowned figure in the medical fraternity.

Patients began pouring in, and we would charge a nominal fee—whatever kept the clinic going, as we were not in it for money. We were in it for service, the development of science and the satisfaction that comes from giving someone a fresh lease of life. This also goes to show that if you focus and strive for excellence, everyone, regardless of rank, faith, caste, etc., will support you. I have always kept my faith distinct from my practice, and so have my supporters. Faith gives me peace and strength, but it is my profession that gives me spark and passion. Passion is important for success in life.

The fact that I went to Aligarh is mere serendipity—I am of the belief that I could have prospered at any other university too. I prospered at Aligarh because it is a good university, not because it is a Muslim university. Both Muslim students and Muslim universities will prosper only on merit, not on the basis of identity. It's that simple! Educational opportunities are available to all youth in India, regardless of faith, but we need to avail ourselves of them. Parents have a huge role to play.

Our community needs a revolution in parenting styles in order to guide kids in the right direction. Youth need to pick up skills relevant not to the present but to the future. If we skill ourselves as per the present, we will end up in petty jobs, but if we want to excel, we have to skill ourselves as per the future needs, thinking as far as twenty years ahead. That is how we can play a part in building a Viksit Bharat by 2047. Even if one must join the family business, let him or her get an MBA and then join the family business, so that they can add value to the enterprise.

The Place of Muslims in a Developed Bharat

India is changing, and with it are Indian Muslims. Not only are the cities witnessing progress, but also the hinterlands. In the last twenty years or so, I have noticed visible changes in my own hometown, Rampur. Hindus and Muslims alike benefit from the general progress of the country. Many local kids have come back after pursuing MD and set up clinics there instead of going abroad or settling in bigger cities. There is also a visible uptick in the number of people living in *pucca* (concrete) houses in my own mohalla (neighbourhood), as the Pradhan Mantri Awas Yojana (PMAY) has been implemented very well, without discrimination. This is a game changer because once durable housing is achieved, a family starts to think about nutrition, education, savings, etc., creating a cohort of first-generation learners.

The Government of India's 'Beti Bachao Beti Padhao' campaign has resonated countrywide among all faith groups, even as challenges remain. It is well known that when assets are scarce, the male child is the preferred recipient of them. Hence, the provision of tangible physical assets has certainly led to an improvement in Muslim families' ability to provide intangible goods such as education, nutrition and healthcare to their next generation, including the girl child. The provision of tangible assets addresses their precarious living conditions, which render them vulnerable to ill health, disasters and the resulting erosion of savings, thereby empowering them to take charge of their destinies.

Reflecting upon the state of the Muslim community today, I'd dare say that our biggest bane is the fact that the least educated and uncredentialed people become imams and maulanas, who then sermonize people blindly, even innocuously, about decontextualized teachings of the Qur'an and the Sunnah. Religious leaders need to contextualize the teachings of the Holy Qur'an and the Hadith as per the present-day world so that our youth are not confused once they enter pluralistic society. There should be some basic qualifications and scientific training required before one can take up the role of a maulana.

Despite being at the cutting edge of civilization, the Islamic world fell behind the western world by about 300 years due to reluctance towards adopting the printing press, which was the source of the European Renaissance. In India, the Mughal period also created a vacuum, as they only promoted poetry and other vices and luxuries. This created historical reasons for backwardness: a lack of role models, a medieval outlook and a lack of social capital among Muslims. Hence, we need to embrace knowledge, new technologies and futuristic skills, and strive for excellence and innovation. Whether we think in altruistic terms or completely selfish terms, all this will empower us as individuals, and also empower our community and our nation.

Our political leaders also need to rise above religion and constituency and think about the nation. For their parochial, localized and short-term gains, they should not indoctrinate entire communities against the majority, as we need to adjust and orient ourselves culturally and become comfortable in modern society with its modern political forms, just as Muslims in the West have adapted to a democratic culture. Muslims in the West live under a uniform civil code, and things like polygamy are unthinkable. Even Saudi Arabia—the wellspring of Islam—is voluntarily embracing reforms such as allowing women to participate in public life, limiting the decibel level of mosque loudspeakers, etc. We need to be reform-oriented, because only those who reform survive.

We need to be comfortable with being governed by a non-Muslim representative and not harbour medieval tendencies for self-rule. After all, it is clear in today's world that Muslims are safer in non-Muslim countries than in so-called 'Muslim' countries that divide Muslims into sects and categories. India, by contrast, is safe for all Muslims, regardless of sect or denomination, giving us both freedom of religion as well as freedom within religion. We are blessed to be in a nation that, despite a bloody partition, maintained a level-headed approach and chose to be a nation for all.

I have travelled the world, and I can say with confidence that the amount of freedom that we enjoy in India as Muslims and as Indians is unmatched. The Gulf countries, Singapore, etc.—though developed—are not democracies and have very strict rules. As for China, we are all aware of how Muslims are confined to detention camps and forced to unlearn Islam. On the other hand, western countries offer a sanitized version of secularism that seeks to purge the public spaces of any display of religion, such as the hijab. I have studied at a minority institution that receives state grants—this would be unimaginable under Western secularism.

Hindus and Muslims need to learn to live like brothers, and it is okay in a household for the younger brother to defer to the elder brother. Just as the older sibling forgives and forgets many transgressions on the part of the younger sibling, so has our great nation moved on from many unfortunate incidents and utterances that poisoned the well since the dawn of independence. Similarly, the younger sibling can also show deference and respect for the elder brother, and we can all live like a family, with mutual love and respect.

I am on the verge of preaching, but Muslims are generally reluctant to listen to someone who does not flaunt a beard, a sherwani, a karakuli* cap and so on. So, my words will be lost on many and may irritate some. That is why I prefer not to preach but to inspire by example. We can inspire younger Muslims towards professional excellence through our deeds, not our words. Today's age is a competitive one, and we need to have Arjun's eye (sharp focus) in order to excel. To share an anecdote from the life of Prof. Ashok Bal, he rejected his own application for leave to attend his daughter's wedding as dean of the faculty, which he had sent in at his wife's insistence! This is the kind of commitment and passion for your profession that it takes to excel.

It's not as if Muslim scientists and professionals are not contributing to various fields. But the problem is that we are known, not through our professionals but through our political representatives or our religious heads. This book can be a step in the direction of demonstrating the range of professions in which Muslims have excelled and inspiring younger members of the community, not by preaching, but by showcasing Muslim role models. I must commend Ms Shehla for

---

*A Karakuli cap is a traditional Central Asian headwear, typically made from the fur of the Karakul sheep. Known for its distinctive curl pattern, the cap is often worn by Muslim men. It was worn by Muhammad Ali Jinnah, the founding father of Pakistan, where it is known as the Jinnah cap.

thinking of doing something like this, as it gives voice to those of us who do not have a voice in how Muslims are portrayed or represented.

As a scientist, I would say that the history of human civilization is based upon technological progress, scientific innovation, research and discovery. Hence, India needs high-tech growth and investment in science and technology. There needs to be greater collaboration between academia and industry so that knowledge has some resonance outside the university. We need an amalgamation of the triad of academia, society and industry or commercial sectors. We still have a long way to go, if we are to catch up with China and the US, especially in STEM. But for that, we need pathbreaking innovation, not rote knowledge and pointless discipline. One of my favourite movies is *Three Idiots*, and I recommend that all educationists, parents and students watch it. For India to be a developed nation by 2047, all of us need to put our creative hats on.

Prime Minister Narendra Modi has championed inclusive development by streamlining processes, digitizing service delivery, ensuring direct access to benefits for targeted beneficiaries and providing innovative schemes for health insurance and generic medicines. He has also championed social reforms that can help us become a better version of ourselves. He is an able leader who has brought India repute on the global stage, resulting in real gains for the citizenry such as the homecoming of eight Navy veterans who were on death row in Qatar, and gaining our trust as a leader. We need to join in his mission of Viksit Bharat 2047 by simply doing our best and by simply doing better for ourselves. Jai Hind!

Let the Amrit Kaal
Be a Buildathon

—Dr Zahir Kazi

- Dr Zahir Kazi is a radiologist, educationist, public intellectual and philanthropist.
- He is president of the Anjuman-I-Islam Educational Trust—a Section 8 company in Maharashtra. Anjuman is a 150-year-old organization comprising ninety-seven institutions imparting education in all streams, from kindergarten to Ph.D. to 1.1 lakh students every year at various campuses. It was founded by freedom fighter Justice Badruddin Tyabji and others.
- Dr Kazi is personally committed to the cause of imparting high-quality education and serves on the boards of other educational organizations

too. He was elected to the Senate of Bombay University, representing management colleges.

- A passionate cricketer, he has also served on the board of the Mumbai Cricket Association (MCA).
- The President of India conferred upon him the prestigious Padma Shri—India's fourth highest civilian award—in the category of education and literature on 26 January 2024, his seventieth birthday!

I was born on 26 January 1954, barely seven years after India got independence from British rule in Ponda, Goa, which was liberated from Portuguese rule much later. Therefore, I have grown alongside our fledgling nation, witnessing its transition from a colony to a constitutional republic, and I am lucky to be now witnessing its rapid transformation into a nation of possibility, positivity and prosperity. My father was a businessman from a very well-respected family which had a culture of giving back to society, and that has been my life's mission too. My story is inseparable from that of Anjuman-I-Islam, a charitable educational institution that I have headed for the past fifteen years, and which has given the most amount of satisfaction compared to any of my for-profit work.

I went to Almeida High School in Ponda and excelled at studies, sports, public speaking, elocution, drama, participating in All India Radio shows and displaying a high moral character. I was selected as the Best All Rounder in my senior year, earning the title of 'Mr. Almeidan'. I got into Goa Medical College (GMC) where I did my MBBS, and I learnt that I was the first local Muslim student in its 100-year history to have been admitted to the college! At times, success is easier if we don't see ourselves in categories of identity, because the sky is the limit for what we can dream of. Had I thought of myself as a minority, I may have tempered my own ambitions and aspirations.

I wanted to specialize in radiology, but since GMC did not offer it, I migrated to Mumbai in 1978–79 and enrolled in Topiwala Medical College for my postgraduation, following which I took up work as a clinical associate at Bombay Hospital, which was the largest private hospital in Mumbai. I had a very successful career there, after which I had the opportunity to work at King Fahad Hospital in Madina, Saudi Arabia, in the department of CT Scan which was a new technology in those days (1984). While the Saudi government was keen on retaining me, I had to return to India after a fascinating year-long stint. With whatever savings I had, I came back, got married and headed to the US for my training in ultrasonography at the Thomas Jefferson University Hospital in Philadelphia.

I also did an MRI fellowship at the University of Pennsylvania before returning to Mumbai and starting work at the newly opened Hinduja Hospital in Mahim.

Along with a few others, I launched ultrasonography (USG) facilities in Mumbai as it was an emerging technology. Since USG was not highly developed anywhere in the world, we were still learning by trial and error. Yet, I could see that the massive benefits that it brought to clinical practice needed to percolate to poor patients too. So, even though it was too early in my career for philanthropic activities, I started visiting charitable hospitals as well. I got a portable USG machine and would visit five to six hospitals and three of my clinics with it, working way harder than I needed to or was expected to at that stage. However, the most satisfying aspect of it was that I was treating 30 per cent of my patients free of charge.

All this earned me a good name, and my patients soon included the Who's Who of Bombay (as it was called at the time)—celebrities, politicians, etc. While two of my clinics were in the posh areas of Bandra and Babulnath Chowpatty, one of my clinics was in an area where most residents had poor socio–economic conditions. Though I had the professional satisfaction of being a good doctor, the moral satisfaction of doing substantial pro bono work and the personal satisfaction of being a self-made man, the events of 1992–93 convinced me that the Muslim community should focus more on education, especially quality education.

I was already a part of Anjuman-I-Islam, Mumbai (AIM) then, and I started out as a board member, getting the highest number of votes at the initial stage. Then I was appointed chairman of Tibbia Medical College. Thereafter, I served as the general secretary of AIM for three years and finally as president of AIM for the last fifteen years. I could have easily settled abroad, built my practice and lived a king's life in any country of my choice, but my family ethic of giving back is what inspired me to stay here, substantially reduce my clinical practice, focus on educating the marginalized sections of society and building my nation. The Padma Shri award bestowed upon me by the President of India made me highly emotional as my decades of service had been recognized by my beloved country.

I feel proud that I am politically a highly conscious individual but a politically non-ambitious person— something that has helped the institution a lot. I am truly blessed that everyone at AIM, from the security staff, teachers and board members to the next generation leaders, are highly dedicated people who see their work not as a job but as a mission. In Urdu, we say 'Pet bhare hue, aur khauf-e-khuda waale hain' (literal meaning: Their stomachs are full, and they fear God). In other words, all of us are content with what we do, convinced that this is what needs to be done and our only ambition is the mission of imparting high-quality education to our students.

AIM is an inclusive organization because it is informed by the legacy of our founders, who were freedom fighters. So, in the truest sense of the word, AIM is a nationalist organization, one-of-a-kind in that it is private but charitable. We cater to those students at the school level, 50 per cent of whom are unable to pay fees and 70 per cent of whom are first-generation learners. It is a very difficult job, but we are fortunate to have a team that is driven and passionate. Almost all faculty members stay on campus beyond working hours. The management also values them for their work and worth, which fosters a respectable environment.

Maintaining the morale and securing the loyalty and sincerity of your team requires having ethical practices in place. During the Covid-19 pandemic, even though we went easy on the students regarding fees, I ensured that the salaries of employees would be credited on the first day of each month. The faculty at various AIM institutions handled the transition to e-classrooms extremely well. In their spare time, they would personally distribute food rations among the less privileged. Things like these earn us the goodwill that we enjoy in society.

As part of our 150-year celebrations, our Industrial Training Institute (ITI) has designed and deployed unique high-end technical courses for deaf and dumb children that cater to all communities. I must add here that while AIM works for the educational upliftment of Muslims, our doors are open to all communities. The way we see it, India is one community and all of us must progress together. Education can be an antidote to fundamentalism, a problem that afflicts all communities, whether we like it or not. If we had to focus on one thing for the next twenty years, this is it.

We are taking seriously developments such as AI and we are constantly updating our curriculum to include courses that cater to the changing needs of the times. We have introduced AI, robotics, etc. even at the school level, and we are working to share our expertise with other schools in Maharashtra. The US ambassador to India, Eric Garcetti, visited Anjuman recently, impressed by the fruitful collaboration between top American universities such as the Massachusetts Institute of Technology (MIT) and our schools and colleges.

Our colleges span almost all streams of higher education, and we only lack a modern medical college, which we are planning on building now. We also work to mainstream our students by encouraging them to participate in international competitions. Our engineering students from Saboo Siddik College of Engineering & Academic Excellence participate annually in an unmanned micro aircraft-making competition* in the US. Our team, 'Team Aerosouls' stood first in micro class design in 2014[1] and second in advance class design in 2015.[2]

Saboo Siddik undergraduate students also distinguished themselves by winning the India

---

* SAE Aero Design.

Innovation Growth Program 2.0 organized by Lockheed Martin, the Indo–US Science and Technology Forum, the Department of Science & Technology Government of India, IIM Ahmedabad and IIT Bombay, by designing a prosthetic arm for amputees that runs using myoelectric technology. The project, known as 'HATH, Hands at Help', aims at increasing the functionality of the existing products while at the same time reducing the cost of prosthetic arms.

In 2018, AIM's Saif Tyabji Girls High School and Junior College (Tyabji High, for short) established an Atal Tinkering Lab with a grant received under the NITI Aayog Atal Innovation Mission. Notably, among 1500 schools in India and fourteen schools in Mumbai, the school was honoured with the opportunity to set up this lab on its premises. Additionally, Tyabji High was selected among various schools in India for the visit of Sweden's royal couple, King Carl XVI Gustaf and Queen Silvia organized by NITI Aayog in collaboration with Stockholm Technical University, where they interacted with students engrossed in various electronics projects.

Tyabji High also seized a remarkable opportunity to showcase their project, the 'Maglev Vertical Axis Wind Turbine', at the Akhil Bhartiya Shiksha Samagam 2023 exhibition, held in celebration of the third anniversary of the National Education Policy (NEP) at Pragati Maidan in New Delhi following a rigorous selection process. Ms Umme Hani Shaikh, a ninth-grade student, and Ms Rushada Ansari, a tenth-grade student, from Tyabji High, had the privilege of interacting with Hon'ble Prime Minister Narendra Modi during this significant event. For India to be a Vishwaguru, all sections of society must come forward and join the mainstream by competing in the mainstream—be it UPSC, CDS, JEE, CLAT, hackathons, international Olympiads and so on.

I could go on and on about the achievements of Anjuman's students, but that will be a separate book! All these achievements show the potential of Muslim students, given the opportunity. Hence, my humble submission to Prime Minister Narendra Modi was that while building vocational colleges, the government should consciously cater to Muslim-majority districts— this is not appeasement, but inclusive development. AIM is only one institution, but we need many more. Having met him twice (at the time of writing), I am convinced that Prime Minister Narendra Modi wants to take all communities along; he believes in inclusive development, and we should support him by coming forward and creatively using the opportunities made available by the government.

I do not believe that there has been appeasement of Muslims in India. The Sachar Committee Report documents various indicators of socio–economic backwardness of Muslims even as late in the day as 2005–06, contradicting the narrative of appeasement[3]. What has taken place can be more appropriately termed tokenism. Giving one self-interested Muslim a ministry or a post does not translate to the upliftment of the community. I am okay with less tokenism, less representation and more substantial work that really empowers the community at the grassroots.

AIM takes great pride in dispelling the misconception that women in India are deprived of education and power. On the contrary, we celebrate the fact that 80 per cent of the heads of institutions within AIM are accomplished women who have made remarkable contributions in the fields of education and community development. Their exemplary work stands as a testament to our unwavering commitment to gender equality and inclusivity.

AIM is one step ahead of our national slogan, going from 'Beti Bachao Beti Padhao' to 'Beti Basao' (settle the girl child). Right from their sustenance and education to ensuring that they are well-settled in life, the girls in our orphanages are looked after with the utmost care and concern. AIM has two orphanages for girls that accommodate 400 orphan girls, one at Versova, Mumbai, and the other at Bund Garden, Pune. These foster care homes not only provide essential needs like food and education but also offer a diverse range of professional courses, including computer education, higher education programmes, entrepreneurship courses, etc. so as to make them financially self-sufficient. We don't stop here; we have the unique distinction of finding suitable soulmates for these girls. The selection is done with the utmost care, and marriages take place only with the final approval of the concerned authorities. All the wedding expenses are borne by AIM.

A crucial aspect of managing an organization as large as AIM is governance. At AIM, we excel in good governance practices, transparency in management, leadership accountability, 360-degree feedback mechanisms, and we never let the complacency of a minority institution mindset, or the tendencies of nepotism set in. We religiously hold our annual general body meetings, prior to which we open up the accounts for audit by all trustees.

We are a not-for-profit organization and a charitable trust, and we do not accept any cash. We have a bottom-up budgeting process carried out by various properly structured boards catering to various silos. The budget is then discussed and consolidated by the forty-five-member governing council. AIM is a self-sufficient organization. We hire through the advertisement process and contract through the tendering process, rivalling the governance models of even publicly listed companies. We accept donations only by cheque. All this ensures that we are the preferred organization for philanthropists looking for a credible organization to support. Some of our schools are eligible for grants-in-aid, but we handhold them in doing the paperwork, as it is a complex process. As a recommendation, I would suggest making the application process easier and bringing funding cycle in sync with the academic calendar.

We are preparing the next generation of leaders through a process similar to that followed in corporate organizations and the military, both of which hone promising people to whom the baton can be passed. We are good people who believe in good governance. During my stint as president, we have also focused on international collaborations with universities such as MIT, exchange programmes, placement tie-ups, etc. We also undertook the challenge of building an alumni network; challenging because AIM is a 150-year-old organization with literally lakhs of alumni. However, we are about to reach the target of building a 1,00,000-strong alumni network, at least half of whom we hope to invite for the 150-year valedictory function, preparations for which are underway as I write this. On LinkedIn, we have managed to build a 9100-strong alumni network for Saboo Siddik College of Engineering alone. We have had alumni meets in North America, UK, etc. where I physically interacted with notable alumni.

We have worked with all governments at the state level as well as the Centre, never letting our own political views jeopardize the future of the organization, as is the case in any well-governed corporate organization. In collaboration with the National Council for Promotion of Urdu Language (NCPUL), we organized an annual Urdu book fair, the Urdu Kitab Mela, in January 2024. During the pandemic, we converted our Unani medical college into a Covid-19 treatment facility on the orders of the government that all small hospitals be converted into Covid-19 centres. Veteran Hindi film actor Amitabh Bachchan contributed two ventilators to it; one of our students from the UK contributed another; my family raised funds for the ICU and we actually started a good Covid-19 facility.

We also ran a Covid-19 vaccination centre from the hospital. Our campus in Panvel, in collaboration with the Maharashtra state government, fed 8000 people a day for more than four months after the lockdown to alleviate the immediate crisis at hand. Some of our faculty members drove migrant labourers to the railway station. We offered up our premises for various other charitable activities during the pandemic. Whenever the nation is in need, Anjuman has and will step up and rise to the occasion.

Great nations like the US, Japan, Sweden, etc. are built on the strength of exceptional private enterprise, original thinking, community initiative, voluntarism and individual effort. We in India need to have more community initiatives, build more institutions and realize the power of private initiative. Governments should, theoretically speaking, do more, but if we as a nation remain dependent on government, we will never mature and will always remain backward. Today, we have AIM because someone decided 150 years ago that it was needed. They did not wait for the government to build it.

We need to think of the coming twenty-five years—the Amrit Kaal of India's post-independence journey—as a 'buildathon' where we compete and cooperate, where we undertake private initiative, invent, build, create, imagine, and dream. We must support our leadership in realizing the glorious vision of a Viksit Bharat in its pursuit of making India a *vishwaguru* (world leader). These are not mere slogans. We will make them possible, fill them with colour, texture them with our imagination and add a finishing touch of patriotism. We will put in the labour of love and make our nation reach ever greater heights. We will improve ourselves and build our own capacities so that we may realize our full potential. Let this be our pledge for the years to come.

Reflections of a Diplomat

—Dr Ausaf Sayeed

- Dr Ausaf Sayeed is a former Indian diplomat who served as ambassador of India to Saudi Arabia and Yemen.
- He has also served as the high commissioner of India to the Seychelles.
- He has served as consul general of India in Chicago.
- He has served as secretary (CPV & OIA)* in the Ministry of External Affairs, Government of India.

As I sat down to pen this essay, sipping a cup of freshly brewed coffee on a bright, sunny morning at my residence, my mind started pondering over my journey

---

*Consular, Passport, Visa and Overseas Indian Affairs.

of more than three decades as an Indian diplomat and the numerous memories associated with each of the places of my posting.

Born into a middle-class literary family in Hyderabad, I was under constant pressure from my parents to achieve academic excellence, do something worthwhile in life and make the family proud.

The paternal side of my family traced its roots to Hadhramaut in Yemen; my grandfather served as a state financer for the Sultan of Mukalla. On the maternal side, my grandparents hailed from Surat, Gujarat, but migrated to Hyderabad when my grandfather chose a career in the judiciary and was eventually appointed as a sessions judge.

My father, Awaz Sayeed, was an acclaimed modern short-story writer in Urdu and worked for the Food Corporation of India (FCI). While he remained engrossed in his literary pursuits, my mother, Kaneez Fatima, a working woman and a librarian by profession, took upon herself the mantle of the educational needs of my younger sister and me. She enrolled us in a reputed Catholic school in Hyderabad to help build a strong foundation for us.

I preferred to be financially independent rather than lean on our limited family resources. Soon, I started tutoring school students while I was still in junior college. As a slow-blossoming student in high school, I saw myself transform into a meritorious student, a topper and a gold medallist at the university.

My career goals, however, kept shifting from doing scientific research to becoming a geologist, culminating in an aspiration to be a civil servant.

So, when it came to the preparations for the civil services entrance exam, I had to remain content with self-study or free coaching that was being offered to students from minority communities, as joining a coaching institution of repute seemed beyond my reach. My performance at the free coaching institution was noticed by a teacher who became my mentor. He gently pushed the idea that I should move out of the 'minority syndrome' and advised me to work harder and elevate my performance to become competitive at the national level. With a combination of perseverance, hard work and a shade of luck, I was selected for the Indian Foreign Service (IFS) in 1989, with geology and geography as optionals.

Indeed, the exam takes you through the grind long enough for you to discover or re-discover your inherent talents or weaknesses. In my case, it embellished my penchant for writing, which I have pursued since my college days, by writing articles for science magazines. In 1990, while undergoing training at the Foreign Service Institute (FSI) in Delhi, I published my first book, *Objective Geology*—a guidebook to help aspirants of civil services like myself. I went on to publish a couple of more books on Indian art and culture, as well as a compilation of the Urdu literary works of my father.

I believe the IFS offers an exceptional professional career that provides a vast canvas where you can define your goals, set targets, develop innovative ideas and concepts and execute them, thereby not only achieving immeasurable success and recognition but also deriving personal satisfaction. My career as a diplomat provided me with a rare opportunity to travel across continents and discover new societies and cultures, from Egypt, Qatar, Saudi Arabia and Yemen to the Seychelles and Denmark.

From an early stage in my career, I was involved in serving people directly in my assignments, including as the regional passport officer (RPO) in Hyderabad, the consul (Hajj) and the consul general in Jeddah, Saudi Arabia. My experience working as the RPO in Hyderabad was very unique. I joined the office in May 1993, a turbulent period post-Babri Masjid demolition and the Bombay riots.

The passport office in Hyderabad, being the only office in united Andhra Pradesh, was always under heavy workload pressure. It had become notorious for issuing passports to several nefarious gangsters and even foreign nationals, all out there to foment trouble in our country. As I started probing deeply into such bogus applications, it turned out that there was a well-established nexus involving some passport office employees, low-ranking police officials and even some civil servants who had facilitated the expeditious grant of passports to such applicants by issuing special verification certificates.

So, my foremost priority was to crack down on spurious applications, weed out corruption, simplify procedures and make the process of obtaining passports less cumbersome for the people. Each day, I would meet at least 500 applicants and try to resolve their grievances, while at the same time tightening the screws on brokers and touts. While I received much appreciation from the general public at large, the vested interests ganged up against me and started intimidating me, but I continued undaunted with my mission.

I was taken by surprise when, at the Regional Passport Officers' Conference in Delhi, the then joint secretary (personnel), Shri E.S.L. Narasimhan, who went on to become the Governor of Telangana and Andhra Pradesh, publicly acknowledged my efforts in streamlining the passport services and curbing the issue of passports to criminals and nationals of some of our neighbouring countries, which he said was having an impact on our national security. After so many years, I still come across people who share pleasant experiences of their interactions with the passport office during that period.

I landed in Jeddah in January 1995 to assume charge as consul (Hajj) and got instantly involved in the preparations for Hajj 1995. Hajj is a very complex 'man-management'* exercise involving interactions

---

*I use the term 'man-management' because the exercise involves managing 1,75,000 hajis over a period of thirty to forty days.

with multiple entities both within India and in the Kingdom of Saudi Arabia. My primary task was to ensure that all essential arrangements were put in place for the comfortable spiritual sojourn of Indian pilgrims to the holy cities of Makkah and Madinah. I was charged with spiritual fervour at the very thought of contributing to this holy affair.

Fresh from my Hyderabad experience, I started monitoring every aspect of the Hajj management minutely, looking at things critically and not being convinced by what appeared to be normal on the surface. I soon realized that there, too, were many devious elements who tried to exploit the Hajj arrangements for their personal gains. It took a great deal of courage and determination to counter them to ensure that arrangements made by the Indian Hajj Mission were not compromised in any manner.

The Saudis regarded India as one of the pioneers in Hajj management, appreciating our focus on planning, detailing, training and digitization. They were mindful of the fact that the Indian Hajj management is quite distinct from that of other countries, as our Hajjis are not a homogenous group but come from different socio–economic backgrounds, speak different languages and have distinct culinary habits. Indeed, India or Bharat can be described as the 'epitome of the world' or an 'ethnological museum' with endless diversity, underneath which lies the continuity of our timeless civilization.

There was, however, one piquant situation when a former external affairs minister of India, while on an official visit to Riyadh, boastfully mentioned to Prince Saud Al Faisal, the then Saudi foreign minister, that 'India is the only country in the world that offers "subsidy" to its Hajj pilgrims.' Prince Saud Al Faisal was amused and interjected immediately, stating that there seemed to be some confusion among the Muslim scholars of India in their understanding of financial affordability and physical well-being as the necessary conditions for intending pilgrims to perform Hajj. He added that Hajj is not compulsory if those conditions are not fulfilled, implying that availing subsidies for performing obligatory Hajj defies Islamic principles. He even offered to send some Saudi Ulema to India to engage in discussions with their Indian counterparts on the subject to dispel any possible wrong notions.

This subject was so sensitive in India that any suggestion to initiate reforms in our Hajj management would be looked upon with suspicion and discouraged. Indeed, some parliamentarians did try to explore alternate financial models for Indian Hajjis based on Malaysia's 'Tabung Hajji' model, but with little success. After several decades, adjudication by the Supreme Court in 2012 deemed the Hajj subsidy not only unconstitutional but also inconsistent with the teachings of the Qur'an, leading to the gradual discontinuation of the practice[1]. Ironically, the prime beneficiary of this 'Hajj subsidy' was, in fact, Air

India rather than the pilgrims themselves, as almost the entire amount of the subsidy was spent on air travel to the holy cities, which was invariably highly priced.

I remained associated with Hajj management for over twenty-five years in different capacities since 1995 and played a pivotal role in the implementation of all innovative policies and schemes of the Government of India, including allowing women to perform Hajj without male guardians. I derive immense satisfaction from the fact that Hajj 2019, which I handled as ambassador of India to Saudi Arabia, had 2 lakh pilgrims from India—the largest ever in our history, thanks to the increase in our Hajj quota by the Saudi Crown Prince Mohammad Bin Salman at the request of Prime Minister Narendra Modi.

I've been interested in cultural diplomacy since the early days of my career, so I got involved in the projection of 'soft power' associated with India's rich art, culture, heritage and spiritualism as I believed them to be an important tool in promoting bridges of understanding between peoples and civilisations.

I was deployed as third secretary at the Maulana Azad Centre for Indian Culture in Cairo when it was inaugurated in 1992. Young and old Egyptians were fascinated by the Hindi language and yoga classes offered by the centre. Most Egyptians were die-hard fans of Bollywood movies and were eager to learn the Hindi language to understand our films better.

In Riyadh, we built a beautiful embassy building, which had a fully equipped mini theatre that was regularly used to screen Hindi movies. In 1997, while posted in Riyadh as first secretary, I curated a film festival titled 'Satyajit Ray: In Retrospect', a week-long film festival of the renowned director. My passion for films encouraged me to persist in showcasing Indian movies in Saudi Arabia when I returned for the second time in 2004 as consul general in Jeddah.

The first 'Asian Film Festival' in Saudi Arabia, held in February 2008, was initiated by me under the umbrella of the Asian Consuls General Club (ACGC), which I had helped establish in 2005. The festival was inaugurated by the then Saudi deputy minister of culture and information for international cultural relations, Dr Abu Bakr Bagader, and opened with a Saudi documentary followed by the Indian film *Chak De India*. Hosting the Asian Film Festival was a pioneering step in an otherwise conservative country that had banned feature films for over three decades until cinemas were allowed to open in April 2018. Screenings of Indian movies in theatres and the annual Red Sea International Film Festival in Jeddah since its launch in 2019 are now regular features as are Bollywood shows across the country.

Earlier, I had successfully experimented with hosting Indian cultural festivals in Qatar and Saudi Arabia. In 1999, I hosted the first 'India Week in Qatar' in association with the National Council of Culture,

Art and Heritage in Qatar, which received all-round appreciation. Then, I organized the first-ever three-week 'India Festival in Jeddah' in September 2005 in collaboration with the mayor of Jeddah.

Cultural and people-to-people contacts have been the strongest pillars of India's relationship with the Arab world. Arab traders started settling on the Malabar coast and other parts of India in the early Islamic era. Likewise, many Indians travelled to different parts of the Arab world, including Saudi Arabia, and settled down, becoming a part of the local milieu. Thus, when I mooted the idea of forming the 'Saudi–India Friendship Society' in 2006, it found instant support from the then Saudi Ministry of Information and Culture, which agreed to patronize it. I collaborated further with the Saudi side to organize the first 'Saudi–India Civil Society Dialogue', when a composite civil society delegation from India visited Jeddah and interacted with a cross-section of Saudi men and women.

The visit of the first all-women Saudi student delegation, comprising fifty girl students from Dar-Al Hekma College, on a week-long educational and familiarization trip to India in February 2007 during my tenure as the consul general in Jeddah, was another ground-breaking moment in our cultural contacts with the Kingdom. The Saudi girls had an extended interactive session with the then President of India, Dr A.P.J. Abdul Kalam, and visited several key institutions, including IIT Delhi. It was no less than a 'cultural coup', as the country was still conservative, and the visit of Saudi college girls outside the Gulf was beyond imagination.

The growing popularity of yoga in Saudi Arabia is another salient aspect of our cultural and people-to-people engagement with the country. The journey of yoga in the Kingdom of Saudi Arabia began a couple of decades ago when some yoga enthusiasts began practising yoga publicly, albeit in a severely restrained manner owing to local sensitivities. Yoga received a major boost in Saudi, when it received formal recognition as a sporting activity in November 2017. This has allayed the misplaced fears among many in the Muslim world that the practice of yoga is incompatible with the tenets of Islam and given confidence to Muslim yoga practitioners around the world. In 2021, while I was serving as India's ambassador in Riyadh, the Saudi Ministry of Sports prescribed formal yoga standards and guidelines for practising yoga and Saudi Arabia became the first country in the Islamic world to enter into a memorandum of understanding (MoU) with India on yoga. My efforts to popularize yoga in Saudi Arabia were recognized by the S-VYASA* University, which conferred on me the prestigious 'Yoga Mithra Award'.

Politically speaking, the year 2006 was perhaps the first turning point in bilateral relations between India

---

* Swami Vivekananda Yoga Anusandhana Samsthana.

and Saudi Arabia when His Majesty King Abdullah
bin Abdul Aziz Al Saud undertook a state visit to
India in January that year as chief guest for India's
Republic Day, the first such invitation extended to a
Saudi monarch. Much of the programme for the visit
was finalized in Jeddah, as it was customary at that
time for the Royal Court to shift temporarily to Jeddah
during the Ramazan and Hajj seasons. This allowed
me to work closely with the ambassador to make
the visit memorable. Indeed, the 'Delhi Declaration'
signed in January 2006 laid the foundation for a
prospective 'strategic partnership' between India and
the Kingdom of Saudi Arabia, which became a reality
thanks to the wise and pragmatic leadership of Prime
Minister Narendra Modi, during whose landmark visit
to Riyadh in 2019, a 'Strategic Partnership Council'
was established between the two countries. At that
time, I was serving as India's ambassador in Riyadh
and was closely involved in working out this strategic
partnership.

This burgeoning relationship between India and
Saudi Arabia was further consolidated during the visit
of Crown Prince Mohammad Bin Salman to India in
September 2023 on the sidelines of the G20 Summit
when I was serving at the headquarters as secretary
(CPV and OIA), holding the responsibility of all
the Gulf and WANA* countries. One of the most

* West Asia and North Africa.

significant outcomes of this visit was the hosting of the summit meeting of the 'Strategic Partnership Council' and the renewed commitment made by Saudi Arabia to invest in India's hydrocarbon and other sectors.

The decision made during India's G20 Presidency to establish the India–Middle East-Europe Economic Corridor (IMEC) provides an excellent opportunity for India to engage with Saudi Arabia, UAE and other countries in the Middle East for mutual economic benefit and prosperity.

When I was posted in Yemen in September 2010, I was the youngest Indian ambassador in any country. I have always been fascinated by Yemen, the country of my forefathers and the land that was considered to be blessed. I could not hide my delight when I received my appointment orders! I was, perhaps, the first person of Hadhrami origin to be appointed as ambassador of India to Yemen, although we did have an Indian ambassador in Riyadh who was also of Yemeni origin.

There are many reasons why India and Yemen, particularly Aden, have strong historical and cultural ties. Aden was a part of British India for 98 years until it became a crown colony in 1937.

Being the closest port to Mumbai, it acted as a gateway to the Red Sea and the Suez Canal, making it a favourite destination for many Indian national leaders and revolutionaries to stop by on their way to or from Europe and other destinations. Netaji Subhash Chandra Bose made two historic visits to Aden, first in

1919 and later in 1935.[2] Mahatma Gandhi visited Aden in September 1931 on his way to London to participate in the Second Round Table Conference, accompanied by Pandit Madan Mohan Malviya, Sarojini Naidu and others.[3]

The British used Aden as a second 'Kala Pani' after the Andaman and Nicobar Islands to incarcerate Indian freedom fighters. An Indian revolutionary named Vasudeo Balwant Phadke was confined here until he died in 1883[4].

Aden was a flourishing port and an important trading centre, attracting a large number of Indian traders, mainly from Gujarat and Maharashtra.

There was a rich heritage of Hindu, Jain and Parsi temples in Aden, with one temple—the Mataji Maharaj Temple—still in active use. I was instrumental in rescuing the Shree Swetamber Jain Temple from illegal occupation by some miscreants who had taken advantage of the crumbling law and order situation in Aden following the 'Arab Spring'*. I ensured that a team from the Archaeological Survey of India (ASI) visited the temple, documented all its ancient scriptures and other artefacts and gave recommendations for its restoration.

---

*The Arab Spring refers to a series of popular uprisings and protests that swept across the Middle East and North Africa beginning in late 2010. These movements primarily aimed to oust authoritarian regimes, address socio-economic inequalities, and demand political reforms.

Yemen also holds a place of special significance for two important religious groups: the Dawoodi Bohras, or Ismailis, and the Parsis. The Bohra sect, which originated in Yemen, shifted its headquarters to India in 1567 A.D. While the Parsis, who had consecrated the 'Holy Fire' at the Adenwalla Agiary in Aden in 1883, shifted it to Mumbai nearly a century later, fearing persecution at the hands of the communist regime in south Yemen.

Indeed, the fascination with Yemen was so great that it could even attract the acclaimed and beatified Mother Teresa to visit thrice. She was baffled when presented with a 'Sword of Honour' by the Prime Minister of Yemen[5] and her friend and priest Edward Le Joly quipped, 'What? A sword is presented to a woman of peace!'[6]

I remember when I called on the then President of India, Smt. Pratibha Devisingh Patil, and she mentioned that the Government of India could expect a greater degree of contribution from me, referring to my Yemeni roots, which I presume she would have seen from my bio-profile. At the time of presenting my credentials to the then President of Yemen, Ali Abdullah Saleh, he remarked, 'I extend a "double" welcome to you in Yemen. First, as the ambassador of India accredited to Yemen, and second, as a person of Yemeni origin returning to his homeland.' Indeed, I was extremely lucky to start my assignment with such words of encouragement from the top leadership of both countries.

Functionally, this helped me tremendously during my stint in Yemen, as the receptivity of government officials and the people was very high. They did not consider me a foreign ambassador, but one of them. I was able to make high-level contacts with comparative ease, both within and outside the government. Both the then interim President of Yemen, Abd-Rabbu Mansour Hadi, and Prime Minister Mohammed Salim Basindwa, with whom I was in regular touch, were keen to strengthen ties with India. In particular, Prime Minister Basindwa would remind me frequently that Dhirubhai Ambani was his neighbour in Aden, and Mukesh Ambani, who was born in Aden, maintained close contact with him. He stated that he wanted to come to India for an official visit and explore possibilities for many strategic collaborations between Yemen and India. The then minister of Transport and Ports, who was an alumnus of Pune University and a strong Indophile, even went to the extent of offering the ancient port of Mocha, overlooking the Bab Al Mandab, and the strategic island of Socotra for management to India! Things would have been geopolitically much different if our establishment of the day had displayed a long-term strategic vision to capitalize on such goodwill.

My first ambassadorial assignment was also beset with severe challenges in the aftermath of the Arab Spring of 2011. My biggest task was to arrange for the smooth evacuation of hundreds of stranded Indian nationals from different conflict zones in Yemen amid a complete security breakdown in the country. We went about the task in a systematic way as per the contingency and security plan chalked out earlier. I ensured that the Indian Embassy remained open throughout the conflict even though embassies of most other countries had closed down and we suffered attacks both on the Indian Embassy and the India House. Our efforts were recognized by the ministry, which recommended my name to the DOPT* as one of its three nominees for PM's Award for Excellence in Public Administration, although the honour was eventually bestowed on our ambassador in Libya, Ms Manimekalai Murugesan, who had also faced an equally challenging situation.

For most of my early diplomatic career, I worked as a commercial officer, either with an independent charge or as an additional responsibility. In this capacity, I strived hard to enhance India's brand image abroad, promote India's exports and encourage inward investments. I was instrumental in launching and mentoring nearly a dozen business groupings and professional networks in the Gulf countries so that these bodies could supplement the work done by the commercial sections of the embassy. Some of the organizations that I founded include: Indian Business Network (IBN), Professionals of India, Saudi Arabia (POISA), Saudi–Indian Business Network (SIBN),

---

* Department of Personnel and Training.

Saudi–India Healthcare Forum, Indian Engineers' Forum and Indian Education Forum in the Kingdom of Saudi Arabia; Indian Business and Professional Network (IBPN) in Qatar and the Yemen–India Business Council in Yemen, besides revitalising the US–India Chamber of Commerce in Chicago. Many of these organizations still remain active.

After this, I took charge as the consul general of India in Chicago and served in this position from 5 August 2013 till 21 January 2017, being responsible for nine states of the US Midwest, which together constituted a region of great significance for India from the perspectives of trade, tourism, investments and cultural and educational collaborations.

Historically speaking, India and the US Midwest had several diverse and deep-rooted connections. Swami Vivekananda's electrifying address before the first World Parliament of Religions held on 11 September 1893 in Chicago; the visit of the acclaimed Jain scholar Virchand Gandhi, who incidentally is regarded as the first Gujarati to visit USA and who represented Jainism at the same event; the famous exchange of communication between Mahatma Gandhi and George Washington Carver during the height of India's freedom movement; Norman Borlaug's contribution to the 'Green Revolution' in India; the association of the Nobel laureate Rabindranath Tagore with Urbana-Champaign and that of the 'Father of India's White Revolution', Dr Verghese Kurien, with the Michigan

State University and of the Nobel laureate Dr Har
Gobind Khorana with the University of Wisconsin-
Madison and lastly, the visit of the then Vice President
of India, Dr Zakir Husain, to participate in the
centenary celebrations of the University of Michigan
on 29 April 1967 amid hectic election campaigning in
India only a few weeks before he went on to become
the third President of India, and the country's first
Muslim president on 13 May 1967 all point towards
the existence of strong people-to-people engagement
between India and the US Midwest since a long time.

The region was diverse, and each of the nine states
in my jurisdiction had their own inherent strengths and
offered great potential to India. I was able to capitalize
on these complementarities to establish 'Smart
State' partnerships between Illinois and Telangana
to accelerate the progress of both parties toward
emerging smart state technologies.[7] I also worked on
building similar partnerships between Maharashtra
and Michigan[8] and between Haryana and Iowa[9]. I was
closely involved with several important educational
collaborations between Indian universities and their
US counterparts.

On the cultural front, I launched an annual cultural
festival called 'Kala Utsav' (Art Festival), which
became very popular. I also lent my strong support to
the annual literary festival 'Eye on India' as well as to
the South Asian Film Festival. On the sports front, I
negotiated the hosting of annual polo matches between

the Delhi Polo Club and the Oak Brook Polo Club, in collaboration with the mayor of Oakbrook.

It was also during my tenure that we successfully retrieved two rare artefacts from a US national—a tenth-century sandstone dancing Ganesha from UP and a fourth-century terracotta idol of Lord Vishnu from the Gupta period—and handed them to the ASI.

Despite my long diplomatic career spanning thirty-four years, I did only two stints at the Ministry of External Affairs (MEA) headquarters in New Delhi, besides the time spent at the FSI as a trainee officer. In my first stint, I served as joint secretary (West Africa) from 2008 to 2010 and contributed to expanding and strengthening India's political and economic relations with twenty-five west and central African countries. Another significant aspect of this assignment was the implementation of the pan-African e-Network Project in forty-seven African Union countries for tele-education and telemedicine.

The last assignment of my career was as secretary (CPV and OIA), in which I was responsible for all consular matters and all issues relating to the Indian diaspora, besides overseeing India's overall relations with countries in the Gulf, West Asia and North Africa.

I always considered the Indian diaspora a great source of strength and support for our country's diplomatic missions and tried to maintain close engagement with NRIs (non-resident Indians) or PIOs (persons of Indian origin) at the grassroots level wherever I was posted. The overwhelming success of the seventeenth Pravasi Bharatiya Divas Convention in Indore, Madhya Pradesh, in January 2023, was a matter of deep satisfaction to me.

Likewise, on the foreign policy front, the Egyptian President Abdel Fattah El-Sisi's visit to India as chief guest of the Republic Day celebrations in January 2023, the return visit of Prime Minister Narendra Modi to Egypt in June 2023 and the visit of the Crown Prince and Prime Minister of Saudi Arabia, Mohammed Bin Salman Al Saud, in September 2023 after participating in the G20 Leaders' Summit, were some of the many high points in our bilateral relations with the Arab and Islamic countries during this period.

I would not have been able to discharge my responsibilities effectively without the strong support and understanding from my wife, Farha, and my three sons, Faateh, Faaleh and Azhaan, despite putting up with frequent dislocation and disruptions as a result of my postings to different countries. Farha also lent a helping hand in our cultural outreach while heading the association of spouses of all ambassadors, both in Yemen and Saudi Arabia, as well as numerous other activities involving ladies of the Indian diaspora.

I owe a great deal to the IFS for providing me with a plethora of opportunities for learning throughout my career. I shall always remain indebted to it.

Bridging Worlds: My Journey as an Indian Muslim Scholar in International Relations

—Dr Sana Hashmi

- Sana Hashmi, PhD, has been a Taipei resident since 2020. She is a fellow at a Taipei-based think tank, the Taiwan–Asia Exchange Foundation and the Houston-based George H.W. Bush Foundation for US–China Relations.
- In India, she has worked with the Ministry of External Affairs and a number of think tanks. She earned her PhD and MPhil from the School of International Studies, Jawaharlal Nehru University, and her master's degree from Jamia Millia Islamia.
- She has authored a book titled *China's Approach Towards Territorial Disputes: Lessons and*

Prospects and is currently working on her second book on India-Taiwan relations. She has over 150 publications to her credit.

(Views expressed here are personal.)

Indian Muslims are not a monolith; they encompass a myriad of identities, and I, as an Indian Muslim woman, am no exception. By profession, I am an international relations scholar with expertise in foreign policies of China and Taiwan. Having studied in India and now living and working in Taiwan, I embrace the richness of my cultural heritage from my home country (India) while navigating the nuances of my adopted home (Taiwan). I see my journey as a bridge between cultures, a defiance of conventions and an infusion of diversity into the field of international relations, which is traditionally considered an elite profession. Living at the crossroads of various identities, my experiences in Taiwan reflect the amalgamation of my Indian heritage, Islamic roots and academic pursuits.

My formative years were spent in the historic streets of Old Delhi. Raised in a devout Indian Muslim family, my identity was deeply influenced by both my religion and my country. My roots are deeply intertwined with the rich religious and cultural heritage of Islam, as well as the fervent patriotism that defines India. The values imparted by my family and the vibrant community that surrounds me have cultivated a profound love for my country. From my earliest memories, I have observed the joyous celebrations of India's Independence Day and Republic Day within my family and neighbourhood, instilling in me a strong sense of national identity from a young age.

To me, the dual identity of being both Indian and Muslim is a source of immense pride. As a member of the Indian Muslim community, I firmly believe that we contribute positively to both our community and the nation at large. Rather than being burdens, we enrich the tapestry of our country with our diverse perspectives and experiences, adding significant value to its rich cultural landscape.

My journey as an Indian Muslim woman from Old Delhi striving to carve a path in academia may or may not be extraordinary. However, when considering the Indian Muslim population, I envision that sharing my story and perspectives could pave an extraordinary path for young Indian Muslims, inspiring them to empower themselves and contribute to uplifting the community. Additionally, I believe that sharing my story could inspire many young Indian Muslims, particularly women who dream of pursuing an academic career. By embracing my varied identities, I hope to contribute to breaking barriers, fostering understanding, and encouraging a celebration of diversity in both personal and professional spheres.

Rising India: Carving Out Space for Indian Voices

Pursuing a career in international relations diverged from the norm for many in India, especially for someone whose upbringing was not steeped in discussions of the shifting geopolitical landscape. Yet, when I reflect on it in 2024, I find myself on an exhilarating journey, breaking barriers, defying conventions, and embracing the changing times. Being called the second ambassador of India to Taiwan by Taiwan's foreign minister Joseph Wu and being commended for my contributions in fostering India–Taiwan relations marked profoundly meaningful moments, underscoring the remarkable trajectory of my life as an Indian Muslim woman in foreign policy.

As the first PhD holder in my family, I am resolved not to be the last. This resolve defines my academic journey, fuelled by a dual commitment: to empower my community and to make academia an accessible path for Indian Muslim youths. My doctoral journey, specializing in Chinese Studies, commenced with a profound interest in Tibet, ignited during a field visit to Dharamshala in 2010. Later, Jawaharlal Nehru University (JNU) provided a fertile ground for my academic pursuits, renowned for decades as a bastion of inclusivity and opportunity. Despite fallacies branding JNU as a hotbed for secessionist ideologies, the reality could not be farther: it is a crucible of critical thought, inclusive dialogue and scholarly discourse. The fact that two of our current cabinet ministers—external affairs minister Dr S. Jaishankar and finance minister Nirmala Sitharaman—are JNU alumni is a testament to its academic rigour and integrity. Like countless other students, JNU exerted a profound transformative influence on my professional trajectory—a sanctuary that not only granted me the freedom to explore but also ignited a deeper fascination with both China and Taiwan.

Almost fourteen years ago, when I commenced my internship at a leading Indian think tank, China garnered considerable interest and optimism, and India-China relations were very different from what they are today. Globally, China was viewed as a vital partner and an engine of growth. Consequently, as I embarked on my PhD journey, concurrent think tank career, and later, my stint with the Ministry of External Affairs (MEA), it was natural for me to generate interest in and develop expertise on China. Subsequent to completing my PhD thesis, publishing a book, and numerous articles, I expanded my research scope to include Taiwan.

Following the 2020 Galwan clashes and China's assertive wolf-warrior diplomacy, India-China relations assumed a more adversarial tone. Witnessing China's aggressive approach towards India prompted a significant shift in Indians' perceptions, scholarly discourse, and governmental attitudes towards China. This marked a pivotal moment in India–China relations, as China transformed from a perceived friendly neighbour to a visibly hostile one. Traditionally, India had approached China with optimism, aiming to shape the Asian century through cooperative relations. However, China's aggressive stance compelled India to reassess its policy and simultaneously overcome hesitancy regarding Taiwan.

Serendipitously, I found myself in the right place at the right time as India began exploring the potential for mutually beneficial relations with Taiwan. Notably, Taiwan had never commanded significant attention in India until then. My journey to Taiwan marked a profound turning point in my life, revealing a glaring lack of awareness among fellow Indians about Taiwan. Through my advocacy and scholarship on Taiwan and India-Taiwan relations, I endeavoured to bridge this knowledge gap, recognizing that there is still much ground to cover. This realization transcended merely scholarly pursuits; it also emanated from personal experiences as an Indian immersed in Taiwanese life.

Taiwan's adept management of the Covid-19 pandemic fostered a sense of normalcy that impressed me deeply. Moreover, Taiwan's robust democratic system struck me as nearly flawless. Many aspects of life in Taiwan resonated with experiences from India, highlighting the imperative for Indians to deepen their understanding of Taiwan. In navigating the complexities of my life and identity, I have encountered numerous experiences that highlight the intersection of

being Indian and Muslim in Taiwan. From celebrating
Eid at home in Old Delhi to participating in Diwali and
Holi festivities with friends from diverse backgrounds,
I have come to appreciate India's cultural mosaic.
Similarly, in Taiwan, I have found parallels between
the values of harmony and respect for diversity. These
experiences have shaped my approach to international
relations and my work, emphasizing the importance
of mutual understanding and cooperation among
communities and countries.

My ability to contribute to the often-overlooked
India–Taiwan relations partly stemmed from India's
increasing significance on the global stage, particularly
as a key player in the Indo–Pacific region. For Taiwan,
forging and enhancing ties with India became essential.
It was within this framework that my scholarship began
to gain prominence. Personally, India's burgeoning
global influence has spurred my focus on India–Taiwan
relations, a cause that has become increasingly significant
to me over the years. As an Indian scholar of international
relations, I take pride in India's expanding influence,
which has provided me with a platform to contribute.
The international relations field, previously dominated by
western scholars and perspectives, is gradually embracing
regional viewpoints. Indian scholars' voices are gaining
prominence, propelled by India's rising stature and its
pivotal role in the broader Indo–Pacific context.

With the assumption of power by Prime Minister
Narendra Modi and the appointment of Dr Jaishankar

as external affairs minister, India's foreign policy has undergone a noticeable transformation. In 2021, Dr Jaishankar highlighted, 'We find ourselves in a different strategic environment. Our stature on the global stage has grown significantly. The world expects more from us and in a globalized era'[1]. This statement showed that India is ready to take up a more proactive role in shaping international relations and setting the tone. With the Modi–Jaishankar duo at the helm, global perception of India has changed positively, and a stronger India is not hesitating from expanding its footprint.

India is now actively shaping its own narrative and projecting its unique story on a global stage. As India's economic and military strength grows, along with its influential role in the Global South*, India's approaches and policies have undergone substantial evolution[2]. This transformation is evident in India's strategic outreach, from leveraging its diaspora to forging new relationships across regions where its presence was previously limited. India has unmistakably emerged as a formidable force on the global stage.

---

* Global South refers to a group of countries and regions generally characterized by lower incomes, weaker economies, and a history of colonialism or dependency on the Global North. It is a socio-political construct rather than a fixed geographical term. It is used interchangeably with terms like 'third world' or 'developing' countries.

Diaspora outreach has evolved into a pivotal component of India's foreign policy in recent years. Since 2014, there has been a discerning approach towards comprehending and acknowledging the contributions of the overseas Indian community. India's foreign policy has been regarded as people-centric. Initiatives such as establishing Pravasi Bharatiya Divas and engaging with the diaspora at the highest echelons of government indicate a significant shift in recognizing their importance and involvement. The MEA has instituted a dedicated division for diaspora engagement to reinforce ties with the overseas Indian community.

The largest contingent of Indians residing abroad is in Islamic countries such as Saudi Arabia, the United Arab Emirates, Oman, Qatar and Kuwait. Notably, a significant proportion of Indians settled in these countries are Indian Muslims. As India extends its outreach in these countries, it underscores the diaspora abroad as a crucial bridge between their country of origin and their adopted homeland. In this light, Indian Muslims have long been regarded as invaluable assets to the country. As integral members of the diaspora, they make substantial contributions to India's diverse cultural landscape and its external outreach.

India is on the rise, and we Indian Muslims also need to rise with the rest of the country. It is only when we make it our responsibility that the entire nation will be united and rise on a global stage. As an Indian based in Taiwan, I consider myself a living bridge connecting India and Taiwan. Strengthening cooperation between India and Taiwan is crucial for my country's interests, and nurturing economic, technological, educational and cultural ties with Taiwan is a key aspect of this effort. Through my profession and commitment to my work, I actively contribute to furthering this objective. Additionally, Indian Muslims living abroad, including myself, serve as torchbearers not only for our community, but also for our nation as a whole.

Charting a Course for Progress

India, home to the world's third-largest Muslim population after Indonesia and Pakistan (Source: Statista), offers significant potential for the success and contributions of its Muslim citizens to the country. However, as Indian Muslims, it is paramount for us to step forward and actively participate in shaping India's growth trajectory. Failing to do so would mean squandering a momentous opportunity. Despite being the second-largest demographic group in the country, the glaring underrepresentation of Muslims in leadership positions and politics persists.

It is a frequent occurrence for both Indians and non-Indians to express surprise upon discovering that I am a Muslim and their first contact from Old Delhi. This surprise often stems from the limited representation and visibility of Muslims in influential roles, as well as my defiance of the stereotypes commonly associated with Indian Muslims. I aspire to witness this change, and I firmly believe that the impetus for change must emanate from within the community. The issue of underrepresentation transcends marginalization; it underscores the urgent need for corrective measures. As a community, it is vital for us to redefine the narrative and strive towards self-empowerment and advancement.

Higher Education is a Must for Indian Muslims

My career in international relations and scholarship are a testament to the transformative power of education. Pursuing a PhD has opened doors I never knew existed for me, highlighting the pivotal role of higher studies in empowering individuals and communities, both socially and economically.

According to the 2011 census data, the literacy rate among Muslims stands at 68.5 per cent,[3] the lowest among all Indian minorities. The Sachar Committee Report brings out the low participation of Muslims, especially Muslim women, in regular employment.[4] Clearly, there is still a considerable distance to cover on the journey towards community empowerment. To initiate a positive transformation, strategic measures must be implemented, both by the government and the community leaders.

For the community to progress, self-transformation and internal reforms are vital. A pivotal aspect of this transformation is prioritizing education particularly that of women. By laying a strong foundation of education for women, we not only empower individuals but also catalyse the upliftment of the entire community. Moreover, fostering inclusivity, promoting skill development, and ensuring equal opportunities for all are essential steps to furthering the community's journey towards empowerment and prosperity.

The Government Needs to Step Up

There are reservations for minorities in some educational institutions, and it is imperative for the community to capitalize on such opportunities. However, the government could be more proactive in fostering awareness of the benefits of communal harmony. India prides itself on its diversity, and as Indians, we cherish this rich blend of cultures. Nonetheless, recent polarisation and rhetoric, especially on social media, tarnish our country's image, often amplified by western media. It is vital to reinforce our motto, 'Unity in Diversity'. Regardless of our backgrounds or beliefs, it is paramount that we unite as one nation, embracing our differences and celebrating our shared identity as Indians.

The government has taken steps to promote social cohesion and dialogue among different religions. For instance, the frequent convening of meetings between Prime Minister Narendra Modi and religious leaders in India sends a message of harmony and also bolsters India's image among Islamic nations, thereby strengthening India's ties with Islamic countries, but more awareness needs to be generated.

It is important for the people inciting hate speech regarding individuals and communities to understand that mainstreaming Muslims is not appeasement but rather a step towards creating an inclusive society. At the grassroots level, there is a pressing need for reforms to integrate communities such as Muslims. Inclusion of underrepresented communities will undoubtedly boost India's social cohesion, thereby contributing positively to the nation.

Changing the Narrative Helps

Several misconceptions persist regarding Indian Muslims, both within the community and in wider society. One significant misconception is the notion that religion conflicts with national identity. For some, the term Indian Muslim is considered an oxymoron. However, this viewpoint is flawed. Many Indian Muslims have made significant contributions to nation-building while maintaining their religious identity, as this book shows.

I believe religion does not inherently contradict the ethos of the country. The preservation of religious identity and national identity has coexisted in the past and could very well continue to coexist in the times to come. Contrary to misconceptions, many Indian Muslims, including myself, seamlessly balance their religious identity with a deep sense of attachment to their country, which is India (Bharat). This misconception often stems from the underrepresentation of Indian Muslims in mainstream narratives and a lack of dialogue and familiarity among the diverse communities within India, which is why this book is such a timely and important contribution.

India is a secular nation where the freedom to practise one's religion is a fundamental right enshrined in the Constitution. The state is neither entitled nor able to restrict an Indian's religious freedom. Similarly, religion is a personal aspect of life that does not impede one's ability to fulfil their duties as a citizen of India. However, in an unfortunate trend, religion, which should be deeply personal, has become highly polarized. Personally, I do not see my religion as an obstacle or limitation. It is essential to distinguish between religious practices and sentiments towards the country. In reality, both should complement each other and work in harmony.

Furthermore, it is important to recognize that this perspective is not merely a misconception but rather a different viewpoint. Muslims constitute 14 per cent of India's population, adding to the country's diverse and pluralistic fabric[5]. With over 200 million Muslims in India, I find the characterization of Indian Muslims as a minority somewhat problematic. The term minority can carry implications of marginalization and victimization, potentially overshadowing the rich contributions of the Muslim community to India's cultural, social and historical tapestry and often emphasizes a victim narrative. If we persist in viewing ourselves as victims and perpetuating the notion that Indian minorities are marginalized without actively working to uplift the community, this conflict will persist indefinitely.

India belongs to All

India, or Bharat, belongs to all its citizens, regardless of their majority or minority status. It is the responsibility of both the government and community leaders to empower both majority and minority communities, fostering a sense of integration. It is equally crucial for various communities in India to perceive themselves with confidence and take proactive actions that contribute to their own empowerment and societal harmony. Unfortunately, this proactive stance has been largely absent from the narrative. Feeling marginalized and victimized only hinders progress and widens existing divides. It is imperative to change the narrative surrounding Muslims in India. We have two options: either continue being perceived as victims or take empowerment into our own hands. I choose the latter.

I can and must be my own saviour. Indian Muslims must recognize that aligning with elements with political agendas or other motives will not lead to their empowerment but only to social, economic, and religious divide and exclusion. My message to fellow Indian Muslims is to seize empowerment for yourselves and be your own saviour, but a crucial key lies in realizing that empowerment starts from within and at home. Integration into mainstream society comes through education, confidence and perseverance. We must debunk stereotypes while preserving both our religious and national identities.

Today's India is different, and Indian Muslims need to adopt a different outlook that contributes positively to the community and the country. This is how I see and perceive myself. Whenever an opportunity arises, I unabashedly embrace my Indian Muslim identity, for it is integral to my being. Navigating life as a Muslim woman in India and abroad has been akin to traversing a rich and intricate tapestry of experiences. Though capturing its full essence proves challenging, for me, it has been a journey brimming with abundant opportunities.

Rather than serving as a limitation, my Muslim identity has been a profound source of strength and resilience. I envision a future where more young Indian Muslims embrace their identities with pride, forge their own paths and are provided opportunities for further integration into the mainstream. Then the diverse mosaic of India will truly be strengthened, reflecting the unity inherent in our diversity.

A People's General

—(As told by Lt Gen. Syed Ata Hasnain to Shehla Rashid)

- Lt Gen. Syed Ata Hasnain served as the corps commander of the 15 Corps in Jammu & Kashmir, a critical and challenging position overseeing military operations in the region.
- During his stint as general officer commanding (GOC), 15 Corps in Kashmir, he pioneered efforts at civil–military cooperation, initiating the '*Ji Jinab*' campaign.
- He is chancellor of the Central University of Kashmir and a member of the National Disaster Management Authority.
- Given his reputation to be a doer, it was not out of place for the PMO when it put him in charge of managing and coordinating the

National Perception during the rescue effort at the Silkyara Tunnel in Nov 2023.

• The story below, as related to me during a two-hour-long interview, focuses on Gen. Hasnain's life story, academic achievements, struggles, lesser-known anecdotes about his life, etc. It also carries his message for Indian Muslims on the need for excellence, tolerance and hard work.

This essay combines biographical notes and autobiographical reflections, both approved by Gen. Hasnain.

Lt Gen. Syed Ata Hasnain is known in Kashmir for various people-friendly policies that he introduced in the execution of counterterrorism (CT) operations, distinguishing Kashmiri people from terrorists and separatists. As a Kashmiri myself, I remember his outreach programmes towards Kashmiri civilians, who have been nothing more than innocent bystanders in a prolonged conflict. His career, family life and personal story are fascinating and tailor-made to be told for the benefit of many who idolize him and to exemplify how passionate patriotic fervour, a sense of commitment and frontline leadership matter in the lives of achievers in the Indian Army. In his humble home office in Delhi, where the interview took place, medals, army decorations and awards were the only décor, telling a story of substance, integrity and humility.

General Hasnain's story begins in 1942, before the Partition of India, when his father, Major General Syed Mahdi Hasnain, was commissioned into the erstwhile Royal Garhwal Rifles. He carried the unit nickname Joe (Joe Hasnain), which stuck to him all his life. His British colleagues gave him this nickname due to his propensity to never accept anything without fully justifying its adoption.* After having fought in the Second World War, his battalion was located in Peshawar at the time of Partition. That is when he learnt that, as a Muslim, he would have to make a choice between joining the Indian Army or the Pakistani Army. He made up his mind about not serving an army that differentiates between people on the basis of religion or a nation whose core founding idea was faith.

Then a young captain and the only Muslim in his all-Hindu regiment, Joe was still unsure whether his family had chosen to stay in India or Pakistan. Yet he had made up his mind, convinced that, despite the initial jubilation, the idea of a faith-based nation was a non-starter. The European nation-states that had started to emerge at this point were based on the idea of common language and culture; there was no evidence of a successful nation–state summoned to existence on the basis of faith, overriding ethnicity, or language, while displacing people from their homeland. Indeed,

---

*Apparently, his unit likened this trait to Joseph Stalin, hence the nickname *Joe*!

merely twenty-five years into Pakistan's existence, the seams began to show, and Bangladesh was born. Joe Hasnain was also convinced that, despite initial hiccups in a heterogeneous nation, India was the one best suited to not just survive but also thrive, as it was based on equal respect for all faiths.

Joe Hasnain's optimism in the idea of India was subsequently rewarded, and he rose to the rank of a general officer in the Indian Army, as did several other Muslims, including his son, Ata Hasnain. Joe became the first Muslim division commander in the Indian Army. His name was also cleared for the rank of lieutenant general, but he had reached retirement age by then. The fulfilment of that dream of attaining the coveted rank would be left to his younger son, Lt Gen. Syed Ata Hasnain. It would be fair to say that the latter's role model and inspiration for joining the Army was none other than his own father.

Although father and son did not have the privilege of serving together in the Army, between the two of them, they have received ten decorations from the President of India and the Army Chief, which is rare for any family in the Army. The great Indian nation has rewarded the family with some of the highest military honours possible, anathema for the advocates of the so-called two-nation theory.

More than a year before the end of British rule in India, Joe Hasnain had been engaged to a woman named Zakia, who lived with her father in Ajmer before

Partition. However, during the Partition, Zakia's family moved to Peshawar, in present-day Pakistan. Coincidentally, this was just around the time Joe Hasnain was moving from Peshawar to Saharanpur. In September 1947, her father wrote to Joe, informing him that they had moved to Pakistan. Distraught, Joe spoke to his commanding officer, Lt Col McLean, an Englishman, who promised to help him travel to Pakistan and bring home his bride.

For a year, Joe and Zakia only exchanged letters, following which Lt Col McLean gave a letter to Joe addressed to Maj. Gen. Tara Singh Bal, the GOC of the Delhi area, a tall personality by reputation who, in turn, rang up his counterparts in the Pakistan Army and broke the ice by cracking some Punjabi jokes, showing the importance of linguistic affinity over a uni-dimensional religious identity. Without any paperwork, Gen. Bal facilitated Joe's move to Peshawar with two air tickets, and his word was honoured by the Pakistani security establishment on the other side. All this was possible because both armies were still functioning under personalities who were essentially comrades and friends of yore.

On 18 August 1948, Joe Hasnain reached Peshawar, Pakistan, and married Zakia, his fiancée of over thirty months, the very next day. As a twenty-two-year-old newlywed, she flew back to India with Joe, leaving behind her family. The Indian Army then became her adopted family. As Joe Hasnain was often posted to places in field areas in his various ranks before he became a general, he decided that both his sons (Ata Hasnain being the younger) should receive a stable education in a reputed school with a hostel facility.

Therefore, he sent his sons to the prestigious Sherwood College in Nainital. He would draw on the Defence Services Officers' Pension (DSOP) every year in order to fund their education, knowing that education is the best investment in a child's future. Indeed, it paid off, as his elder son, Raza Hasnain, became an Indian Administrative Services (IAS) officer and Ata joined the Army—both highly competitive and highly respected fields after both had graduated from St Stephen's College, considered India's Oxford.

Ata Hasnain was fortunate that he won his first ever prize in life from the hands of Mrs Siloo Manekshaw (the wife of India's first field marshal, Sam Manekshaw) when he was in Class 5 at the Defence Services Staff College (DSSC) Children's School, Wellington. Years later, in 1987, when he secured the first position in the research projects of DSSC 42nd course, he received the Lentaigne Medal from the legendary field marshal himself. There was no dearth of inspiration for him to join the Army or do well. However, despite his father's Army credentials and early orientation to the Army, his professional journey was anything but easy, and he had to come up against various odds.

During his initial training as a young commissioned captain, Hasnain sustained a knee injury that relegated him to a 'low medical category' status for three years. While his peers moved from one course to the next, he could not complete his first course. But he used this time to sharpen his military skills, relying on his good education, intellectual strengths and ability to learn quickly from his troops. He was aware that the battalion support weapons (BSW) course would come up in about two and a half years. This would be his chance to prove himself worthy.

So, while Sunday was a day of recreation for other officers, he and his jawans would train on support weapons from 6 a.m. onwards. For two and a half years straight, he trained at the break of dawn every single day for a course that would come up three years later. When he was finally proceeding on the BSW course to Mhow, his CO suggested that he go to Allahabad for some pre-course training to make up for his lack of formal pre-course training. However, Capt. Ata Hasnain sought a chance to demonstrate his expertise to the CO. When he did so, the CO, Col. Dharampal, was shocked. He asked everyone, in disbelief, how that was possible. That was when he learnt that Capt. Ata Hasnain's 'pre-course training' had been going on for years, including weekends!

Col. Dharampal, a war veteran and former prisoner of war (PoW), hugged the young captain and asked him to undergo RCL (recoilless rifle) training on the short leave before the course. At the end of the BSW course, he emerged as the 'Best Student', was awarded a trophy (his most coveted trophy) and never looked back. At times, hurdles may seem like mountains, but we only need a slight shift in perspective to look beyond them. Having a deficit of some kind can and should motivate us to work even harder, harder than all others, and emerge stronger. Capt. Ata Hasnain, as a young infantry officer, could have just given up, as it is not easy to make up for three lost years of Army training, but he had the strength of will, belief in oneself, farsightedness, massive resolve, perseverance, consistency and a positive attitude to stay motivated and focused on his goal.

To have such a huge disappointment at the beginning of one's career means that one couldn't possibly dream of rising to the highest ranks in the Army. However, what people think they lack in one area can be made up by polishing other skills. This is as true for any individual as it is for a community. Whatever is lacking in capability can be made up by using education, excellence, skills, focus and a positive mindset. Often, our biggest fear is not that of failure but of success! Many believe that they are not good enough to deserve transformational success. Hence, they struggle to imagine themselves at the very top. Winners, by contrast, see themselves as capable and deserving; hence, they work towards it. They are not delusional, but they dare to dream—this is what differentiates naysayers from winners. Naysayers enumerate reasons why something is impossible.

Winners demonstrate what is possible, and Capt. Ata Hasnain was born to be a winner.

As he progressed through the ranks, Capt. Ata Hasnain stayed ahead of his peers in every course, gaining a head start while working hard to make up for the initial handicap. Receiving the Best Student trophy in the BSW course set his career path on a trajectory to success. Not only did he ace all subsequent courses, he also demonstrated instructional capabilities, receiving the 'I' grade in various courses. It acted as a major positive reinforcement pathway, training his mind to expect reward only after toil, making hard work exciting. While the Army is a pure meritocracy, this is generally true in life too. People can try to undercut you, sabotage your success and so on, but in the long run, hard work outweighs it all. Those who work hard can never fail. Intelligence, good education, talent, etc. can only take you so far, but beyond a point, hard work and consistency are the traits that truly matter. Even highly intelligent people are outdone by hard workers, as there is no alternative to being industrious in life, not even being a genius.

One of the toughest courses in Capt. Ata Hasnain's training was D&M (driving and maintenance), in which most people failed and in which getting a Charlie (C) was customary. While Capt. Ata Hasnain was undergoing pre-course training for BSW, he also received training for the D&M course with the mechanical transport platoon of his unit, 4 Garhwal

Rifles. An infantry officer getting the AXI grade (highest grade with instructional capabilities) in D&M was unusual, but Capt. Ata managed to add this feather to his cap too. One can say that while trying to compensate for the time lost due to injury, he overcompensated, surpassing all odds. In the BSW course, he received an AXI grade in each of the three legs: MMG, Mortar and RCL. While these are peacetime achievements at a sub-unit level, it is the daily grind of such training that prepares a young officer for war.

Speaking of operations, as a major, Ata Hasnain served with the Indian Peacekeeping Force (IPKF) in Sri Lanka from 1987 to 1990. He also served as a Lt Col and for some time as a full colonel with the UN Peacekeeping Forces, first in Mozambique and later during the genocide in Rwanda in 1994–95. However, before that, he also saw active operations in Punjab during the period 1990-91 and later as CO of his own unit, 4 Garhwal Rifles, at the Siachen Glacier and in easter Ladakh in 1995–96, the scene of the current standoff with China. He was the first Muslim officer to be inducted into MI-1, the Directorate of Military Intelligence section that handles Pakistan. All these assignments led him to rediscover himself and develop leadership and rapid decision-making capabilities.

His experience in Sri Lanka—a staggeringly difficult one at the core of the Liberation Tigers of Tamil Eelam (LTTE) supremo Prabhakaran's lair—led him to rediscover his inner strengths and survivability.

He attributes the quality of camaraderie of his unit officers and the deep sense of loyalty of his soldiers as the reasons for the success of the unit. It was a long journey from there to his appointment as GOC 15 Corps (aka 'Chinar Corps') around 2010–11. The tough insurgencies he had experienced in Sri Lanka, Punjab, on the African continent and many tenures in Jammu and Kashmir had seasoned him into a battle-hardened soldier, adequately trained in India and abroad, and having a sound understanding of strategic affairs. He was posted along the Line of Control (LoC) several times, including in Siachen, and knew the entire geography of Jammu and Kashmir intimately.

Having been posted in the Kashmir Valley at the height of the Kargil War in 1999 as Col. GS (Colonel General Staff) at HQ Victor Force of the Rashtriya Rifles, he handled both north and south Kashmir, understanding the finer nuances of proxy war, local support, networks supported by Pakistan, the role of separatists and that of the media. It was in this period that the nature of conflict changed, with suicide terrorism being increasingly adopted by Pakistani jihadis (also known as *fidayeen*). He drew on all these experiences and learnings during his various stints in Kashmir thereafter, too, including commander of the Uri Brigade and GOC of the Baramulla-based Dagger Division.

As GOC of the 15 Corps, where he moved at the behest of the then Army Chief, Gen. V.K. Singh, Gen. Hasnain brought context to combat. He pioneered the idea that the Indian security establishment needed a calibrated approach depending on the progressive decadal evolution of the conflict. No doubt, the 1990s were a tragic phase of the conflict, which required a higher proportion of kinetic measures—bullets, encounters, you name it. However, after the restoration of democracy in 1996, while sticks continued to be dished out, nobody was handing out the carrots. The soldiers of the 1990s had seen only hostility, mistrust and ambushes. A differentiation needed to be made between the 1990s and the 2000s, stepping into the 2010s.

Lt Gen. Ata Hasnain believed that at conflict initiation, one may use a lot of hard power, but as the situation progresses and success is gained, kinetic power needs to be calibrated and balanced with soft power in a suitable proportion. This understanding represents his lasting contribution. He got inspiration, rigour and motivation from his father and imbibed sensitivity and softness from his mother. This earned him the unlikely accolade of being 'a people's general' from *The Indian Express* no less, which would generally maintain a critical take on Army affairs with respect to Kashmir. The 2000s were not the 1990s, and the 2010s were not the 2000s. Indeed, the 2020s are not the 2010s, as Kashmir has witnessed a sea change in the security situation, even though challenges remain. The security forces have accordingly tweaked their concept of operations and approach to conflict, and the Hon'ble

Home Minister of the country has gone on record to say that the continuation of the Armed Forces Special Powers Act (AFSPA) may be reconsidered, keeping in view the situation.

Gen. Hasnain brought in this nuance when he became the GOC of 15 Corps and reinitiated the 'Ji Jinab' campaign, which was an idea first pioneered by his predecessors and former outstanding corps commanders, Gen. Patankar and Gen. Nirbhay Sharma. Already, in 1997, Operation Sadbhavna had been initiated, which was geared towards winning hearts and minds in Kashmir, an example of military civic action. Yet, it was not sufficient as it did not address the behavioural aspects of the interaction between a soldier and a civilian, which can either breed resentment or respect. Ji Jinab was only a generic term used for orienting soldiers as regards the cultural sensitivities of Kashmir and Kashmiris. It did not mean going soft on terror, but instead establishing a rapport with civilians, winning their hearts, and extending warm gestures to them in a manner appropriate to their culture. As a simple example, it is customary in Haryana to refer to the elderly as 'tu' without it being offensive, but in Kashmir, even peers are addressed as 'aap'. Now, in every job, young trainees receive orientation towards the organizational culture or corporate culture, but no such thing had existed for soldiers.

Hence, 15 Corps started the 'Entry into Kashmir Cadre' as a mandatory orientation for soldiers posted to serve in Kashmir. This would also mean better engagement with the locals in existing outreach programmes like Sadbhavna. Soldiers were also given an understanding of the progression of the conflict and the need to minimize collateral damage while going after the terrorists as usual, keeping the LoC under complete check as regards infiltration, and preventing local recruitment. Gen. Hasnain also renamed 'Operation Sadbhavna' to simply 'Sadbhavna'. as the former sounded more like a military operation than an outreach programme.

Wanting to contribute something innovative and effective, Gen. Ata Hasnain felt the Army needed better communication with the local populace. He thus started another practice termed '*awami sunwai*' (public hearing) initially as a means of involving the civil administration in outreach programmes. The general directed that shamianas be set up and refreshments served to people before starting off the conversation. To quote the general directly:

> At times, we would call an elderly person from among the locals to recite a *dua* (Muslim prayer) before starting off the conversation. Lending an ear to people's woes sent a very powerful message. At the awami sunwais, people opened up about governance problems which we let the civil administration handle. On 12 September 2011, *Outlook* magazine, which is often critical in its orientation, applauded our efforts in a cover story saying that, for the first

time in Kashmir, the Army seemed to be getting it right. That was the biggest reward for two years of sleepless nights and relentless efforts, which saw massive protests. I am proud to have served my nation and the Kashmiri people during this difficult time.

A local Kashmiri journalist once questioned him and felt what he was attempting was nothing more than 'town hall communication', a practice quite effectively used by benign and right-thinking monarchs in the Middle Ages. However, it is important to remember that in those days, when militancy was still at a high level, the civil administration was not in a position to reach remote areas. The Army utilized its capability to reach remote areas to facilitate the civil administration's access to citizens and to address their grievances in the remotest of areas and the toughest of terrain. Militancy and violence restrict the civil administration's ability to address public grievances, creating a governance deficit that can create further resentment, as we have seen in LWE (left-wing extremism)-affected areas. Extremist organizations often use the governance deficit as a pretext to recruit locals and create an ideological justification for violence. Hence, what Gen. Hasnain initiated was more than town hall programmes; it gave a face and a tangible shape to notions such as 'state', 'administration' and 'governance'.

These efforts to integrate the people of Kashmir with the nation have borne fruit over time, and what is seen today in Kashmir is an unprecedented era of normalcy and keenness to be part of the India story.[1] What has helped is a congruence of purpose between New Delhi and Kashmir, which has led to better coordination between civilian administration and the military as well. And today, even though Gen. Hasnain is not in Kashmir himself, he says he completely endorses the government's approach towards the local people. The general further states that the Jammu and Kashmir Lt Gov., Shri Manoj Sinha, has displayed great acumen, mixing with the local people as if he were one of them, reducing the scope for festering grievances to fuel discontent.

The abrogation of Article 370 has finally allowed the fruits of development to percolate to the grassroots level, dealing a death blow to separatism, radicalization, and insurgency. There is a clarity of purpose displayed by New Delhi in its Kashmir policy, which has been difficult for various administrations to achieve due to political, social, religious, and geopolitical reasons in the past. Today, one can see unprecedented events such as mass celebrations on New Year's Eve in Lal Chowk attended by local men and women in minus 5.4°C temperatures. Young Kashmiri rappers singing praises of the nation; former critics and cynics turning around and praising the Army and the nation; people finally realizing that Pakistan is a sponsor of bloodshed, pain and violence, whereas India is a sponsor of peace. It is a deeply emotional moment for men like Gen. Ata

Hasnain who have served in Kashmir, the holy land of Sufis (*reshi-vaer*), to see that their sacrifices have not gone in vain. The people of Kashmir have been relieved of the burden of the conflict that they have borne for decades, and they can now lead normal lives and think about normal things, such as savings, investments, careers, recreation, entrepreneurship and what not.

On being questioned whether this was the final solution and whether he was satisfied with the notion of conflict termination having been achieved in Jammu and Kashmir, Gen. Ata Hasnain spoke at length about his understanding. His words are reproduced below:

> Challenges for us remain: the spike in cross-border terrorism along the Pir Panjal range in 2023 and the continued targeted killings of police personnel, minorities and non-local labourers in the Valley, etc., are desperate attempts on the part of Pakistan to stay relevant. However, we must take a moment to acknowledge, if not celebrate, our achievements. India is not only taking steps to contain insurgency and infiltration at home but also responding properly through military and diplomatic means. One of the things that has helped is the stopping of cross-border trade, which was a vehicle for terror financing through over-invoicing, etc. The government of India has effectively curbed the whole ecosystem of terror, drying out the terror financing networks, terrorist safe-houses and hideouts, thereby reducing

bloodshed, protecting human rights and providing peace and security to the region. Thus, the present political establishment has addressed the social, political, and financial causes behind the violence. It's important to acknowledge all this because this was my thinking behind the efforts for civil-military cooperation during my tenure. Kashmir could not have been solved militarily alone, and the government of India has replaced radicalization with governance, terror with development and bloodshed with hope.

Conflict around the world is associated with violence, and there is usually little to no scope for kindness or humanity. However, I view the conflict as a spectrum. In my efforts as GOC of the Chinar Corps and in the present government's efforts towards welfare and good governance, a nuanced understanding of this gradation is reflected. Today, we see that the Armed Forces Special Powers Act (AFSPA) has ceased to be a matter of debate. During my tenure, that is, the 2010s, the three summers of protest (2008, 2009 and 2010) led to an intense debate about the powers available to armed forces in places declared 'disturbed areas'. I had maintained then, as I do now, that once peace is established and most areas are declared 'non-disturbed', the Army will go back to the barracks, and the matter will cease to be a contentious issue. While it seemed like a distant dream back then, it is slowly becoming a reality, with even the Union home minister acknowledging it as a possibility. The removal of mental barriers like Article 370 has gone a long way in securing peace, at least with respect to local protests and insurgency. As for Pakistan, India will continue to deal with it militarily, diplomatically and politically. However, the biggest challenge—that of putting our house in order—is on the verge of being achieved.

Gen. Hasnain also urged the youth of Jammu & Kashmir to understand the designs of our neighbour by stating,

First, Pakistan sponsors acts of terrorism compelling the Army to launch combing operations, CASO (cordon and search operations), interrogations, etc. leading to resentment among innocent civilians and a boost to 'human rights discourse', which is often a diplomatic tool to weaken India's position on the global stage. The real improvement in the human rights situation has come from India's strong efforts against terror. Civilians are the Army's allies in the fight against terror, and we must fight this menace together. India is a land of opportunities and Kashmiri youth are as much citizens of India as anyone else. There is a need to build bridges and the government is making various efforts to connect people. There are equal opportunities for Muslims in India. I, for example, hold two important assignments even after retirement based solely on my capability and experience, not on any kind of tokenism. If we have something to contribute, there is always an outlet for it, as we are a huge country full of opportunities. My tenure in Kashmir ended in June 2012, roughly a year before my retirement from the Army in July 2013. However, in my mind, I never retired, as I felt that I had a lot to contribute. Over the next seven years, I wrote and spoke extensively on strategic affairs and in 2020, I was invited by Hon'ble PM Shri Narendra Modi to join the National Disaster Management Authority (NDMA). The Indian Army has always been at the forefront of serving people in times of distress or disaster, and I accepted the assignment as a continuation of my military spirit. The high point of my career in the NDMA was the Silkyara Tunnel rescue operation in November 2023, which the entire nation watched with bated breath. Alhamdulillah, we managed to save lives like we always do. I thank the Hon'ble PM for trusting me with the assignment. He had specifically asked that I be involved with the rescue and the projection of the Government's efforts, and I am humbled to have lived up to his expectations.

Gen. Ata Hasnain went on to say,

'I have cited this example in order to make a larger point to young Indian Muslims—any employer will look at your skill, education and experience alone, not the colour of your skin. We should be devout Muslims, but we should not denigrate any other God. We must respect all faiths and participate in the festivities of all other faiths. This is how bridges are built, and this is what makes India a great nation. Tolerance is a two-way street, and it is infectious! Once we demonstrate that we hold other people's faiths in high regard, we will surely see the regard reciprocated for our faith.'

He further stated,

'We must stop thinking in narrow binaries of Hindu, Muslim, etc. As a Muslim, I consider myself a role model not just for Muslims but for people of all faiths. Yet, I would take this opportunity to address Muslim youth and assure them that India is a meritocracy. There is a definite underrepresentation of Muslims in various fields, but I would attribute it more to our lack of awareness and lack of education. To cite an anecdote, I was invited to speak at a madrasa and motivate the students studying there to join the armed forces. I spoke for fifteen to twenty minutes about equality of opportunity in the armed forces, etc. At the end of my talk, a student innocently asked me whether I was a general, to which I replied in the affirmative. But the young man, still confused, asked me, "In which Army are you a general?" I responded with "The Indian Army", trying to answer in as matter-of-fact a manner as possible. At this point, the kid said, "But the Indian Army does not have Muslims; how come you are from the Indian Army?" This reflects the lack of awareness in our own community. While information technology has helped disseminate information, it has also served to amplify disinformation and misinformation. In 2017, I wrote an op-ed in The *Times of India* against a misinformation campaign about there being a Muslim regiment in the Indian Army that refused to fight in the 1965 war against Pakistan[2]. Such misinformation campaigns originate from Pakistan and are intended to create communal disharmony in India, exploiting the slightest of social divisions.'

Gen. Ata Hasnain went on with his passionate description,

'From Enaith Habibullah, who was the first major general in the Indian Army and the first commandant of the National Defence Academy, to Mohammed Amin Naik, who was the first major general from Kashmir in the Indian Army, there is no dearth of Army leaders from the Muslim community. My father was the first major general of the faith to command a division. Muslim lieutenant generals include myself, Lt Gen. Mohammed Zaki, Lt Gen. Zameeruddin Shah, Lt Gen. Sami Khan, the late Lt Gen. Jamil Mahmood and so on. However, there is often less awareness within our own community about them than among other communities. So, while we need to raise awareness about the contributions of Indian Muslims, we also need to educate our own community about them. I have rarely, if ever, been invited to speak at minority institutions and even when I am, the students are not receptive enough, as the things that I have to say do not always suit their expected narrative. That is why I chose to contribute to this book. We need to dispel myths and misconceptions about the Indian Army.'

Concluding his explanation, Gen. Ata Hasnain said,

'When I ask Muslim families to send their kids to the Army, they often respond, saying that in the Army, cadets are forced to drink alcohol or consume non-halal meat. This is absolutely false. If you do not wish to drink, nobody forces you. If the supply contractor is Muslim and the meat is halal, you will be informed about it. If there is a situation where halal meat is not available in the mess, Muslim soldiers are informed about it, and they are given the protein equivalent of the same in the form of eggs or paneer. The calorific value of what is being served to halal eaters is the same as that for everyone else. These misconceptions arise because there used to be a time when rum was issued to soldiers serving in cold weather conditions, but even that practice has stopped now, and there is instead an allowance for the same, which each individual soldier can use according to his or her own convictions. I am trying my best nowadays to break many of these misconceptions. I was fortunate to get great opportunities in the Indian Army and received many honours and awards from the President of India and the Army Chief (eight to be precise), and the country has trusted me with some of the most crucial and sensitive assignments. There has been no suspicion against Muslim soldiers. Yet trust is a two-way process. We also need to take a leap of faith and place some trust in our country and its institutions.'

Faith in Constitutional Ideas Is the Only Way Out

—Prof. Faizan Mustafa

- Professor Faizan Mustafa is an accomplished legal scholar who served with distinction as vice chancellor (VC) at two premier law universities in India. During his tenure of over a decade as VC of the National Academy of Legal Studies and Research (NALSAR), he enhanced the institution's reputation as one of India's foremost law schools.
- He currently leads Chanakya National Law University (CNLU) as its VC.
- Over the past three decades, Prof. Mustafa has produced over 100 research publications and authored seven books, focusing on constitutional law, personal laws, intellectual property rights and criminal law.

- He has also served on various national committees dealing with legal reform.
- His YouTube channel Legal Awareness Web series (LAW's) has over 7,00,000 subscribers and is aimed at educating people about current legal issues in simple language.

My journey began in the small but vibrant city of Moradabad, UP. From the sixth to the tenth grade, I was enrolled in a Christian missionary school, renowned as the best educational institution in Moradabad. However, my initial academic pursuits were anchored in science, a path I treaded until the tenth grade. Despite attending the premier school in the city, I discovered that science failed to ignite my intellectual curiosity. I was indeed weak in science and mathematics.

The pivotal shift occurred when I, on my own, decided to redirect my academic trajectory. Motivated by a growing interest in social sciences, fuelled in part by my elder sister's pursuit of an MA (history), I transitioned to the Government College, which too was quite a reputed institution at that point in time for the eleventh and twelfth grades. Immersing myself in social science subjects, I found inspiration in a remarkable Prof. S.C. Sharma, who taught me history. His engaging and insightful teaching methods laid the foundation for my enduring passion for history.

This transformative phase at Government College not only nurtured my academic interests but also paved the way for my foray into debating. This venture became a defining milestone as I clinched victories in the district championship and commissionerate championship and eventually secured a position in the statewide competition in UP. The competition was fierce, involving thousands of colleges across the state, with only two representatives selected from each district.

This accomplishment held particular significance, not just for me but for the college as well. Although initially hesitant, my mother's approval was secured through a persuasive letter from the principal, emphasizing the prestige associated with my participation. The journey took us to Gorakhpur, marking a singular milestone in my childhood—a testament to the competitive spirit, dedication and profound impact of engaging in intellectual pursuits during the formative years.

I come from a family of academic achievers. Despite the challenging educational landscape for Muslim girls in the 1950s, my mother secured the sixth position in the UP Board. Her remarkable academic prowess, marked by consistently high scores in the 90 per cent bracket, reflected her passion for learning. My father, who had gone to the prestigious Roorkee College, shared this enthusiasm for education, and the household was imbued with a commitment to knowledge.

Education was not just encouraged in my family; it was a core value. My mother, until the age of around eighty-two, was an avid reader, reading about 200 pages a day! However, in 2020, she was diagnosed with dementia, which has been a source of immense sadness for the family. The emphasis on education was not confined to my immediate family but can be traced back to my maternal grandfather, who was also deeply involved in the field of education.

I have one brother and two sisters. My brother went on to achieve success in the civil services, eventually retiring as Secretary to the Government of India in the Department of Agriculture and Food. My older sister excelled in academics, topping the entire university during her master's studies. She superannuated as principal of an inter-college for girls in Lucknow. My younger sister, too, finished her master's and decided to become a homemaker after a few years of teaching. While I may not have matched the academic achievements of my siblings at that time, I eventually found my calling in the field of law in subsequent years.

Despite our family's inherited ancestral properties, our mother instilled in us the value of self-reliance. She emphasized the importance of digging our own well rather than relying on the prosperity of our ancestors. And so we refrained from developing an interest in the family's properties, leading to the unfortunate loss of some assets as others took over! Although my mother expressed regret later, stating that we had not shown enough interest in safeguarding our properties, we adhered to her initial guidance to focus on carving out our own paths in life. Despite the setbacks in terms of property loss, each one of us found success in our respective endeavours.

After graduation, I opted for law, as law is the best profession for any debater, and the law faculty at AMU, prior to the establishment of national law universities, was one of the top three law schools in the country. Securing the top position in LLM marked a significant juncture in my professional journey. Contrary to the conventional path of young law graduates engaging in legal practice, my trajectory swiftly led me into academia. Topping my LLM opened the door to a faculty position, and within a month of completing my master's degree, I was appointed to AMU's law department. While I had qualified for the UPSC civil services prelims, I chose not to take the mains that year.

Unlike the anticipated struggles associated with securing a job, my entry into academia was absolutely smooth, as my supervisor and mentor, Prof. M. Zakaria Siddiqui, was keen to have me on the faculty. But despite the initial ease of securing my first job, I faced unexpected rejections for the position of professor— twice at AMU. Strikingly, both instances unfolded when I was arguably the most qualified candidate. The complex interplay of university politics and subjective decision-making in the selection committee subjected me to this frustrating experience.

The culmination of these setbacks led to a pivotal decision—accepting the offer for the position of registrar when it was extended to me by the university's VC. In hindsight, I recognize this as a strategic misstep, veering away from the academic path I envisioned. The administrative role, while offering its own set of challenges and responsibilities, distanced me from the academic realm.

Balancing administrative duties and the pursuit of academic excellence became a delicate act. The decision to shift focus from academia to administration shaped a trajectory that, in hindsight, reveals both the opportunities and sacrifices inherent in navigating the corridors of higher education. Being an academic administrator may be good for the institution you lead, but on a personal level, it is bad and has a huge personal cost.

Navigating the realms of academia and administration posed a formidable challenge, but drawing inspiration from the stalwarts who shaped my academic journey proved invaluable. In the domain of history, luminaries such as Irfan Habib, Athar Sahib and Shireen Moosvi left an indelible mark on my understanding of the subject. The transition to law, guided by the expertise of my supervisor, Prof. Zakaria

Siddiqui, and eminent professors such as V.S. Rekhi, Ahmed Siddique and Mushir Alam Saheb, unveiled a new realm of passion and dedication.

One noteworthy trait common to all of them was the unwavering commitment of these professors to their craft. Prof. Ahmed Siddique, for instance, exhibited his dedication by arriving a few minutes before the commencement of class, ensuring a seamless transition into the lecture as soon as the bell rang. Even during my tenure as the university registrar, my commitment to teaching remained unwavering. Prioritizing the first period of 8–9 a.m. law class, I would then proceed to the registrar's office.

Upon assuming the role of VC, the commitment to teaching persisted. Continuously engaging in the classroom setting, I found profound joy in imparting knowledge—a sentiment that surpassed the challenges of administrative responsibilities. The passion for teaching, instilled by the remarkable educators and eminent professors, served as a guiding force, propelling me to navigate the intricate balance between administrative duties and academic pursuits.

In the contemporary landscape, characterized by hyper-specialization and cutthroat competition, the ability to seamlessly weave administration and academics becomes a defining attribute in the pursuit of excellence. My success as a VC lies in the fact that I govern the universities from my classrooms, and I involve students in all major decisions.

Advice for Younger Muslims

In offering advice to the aspiring Muslim youth, my reflections draw from the conviction that our nation, guided by a democratic and liberal constitution, provides fertile ground for individual excellence. Regardless of the chosen field, recognition is a natural outcome of genuine proficiency. The spectrum is vast, extending from sports, where individual players have not only excelled but have also led the national team, to the prestigious domain of civil services, where Muslims have been toppers.

Having been intricately involved in the UPSC interview process over the years, I can attest to the advantage that being a Muslim can afford in the interview phase. The predictable nature of questions related to Kashmir, the Uniform Civil Code (UCC), Muslim personal law and issues concerning Muslim women allows for strategic preparation. Contrary to preconceived notions, my experience indicates a welcoming atmosphere during interviews, with boards often encouraging Muslim candidates and affording them ample time to articulate thoughtful responses. Additionally, the relatively low number of Muslim candidates who qualify for the mains exam creates an environment where they can differentiate themselves by drawing on their unique experiences.

Having chaired selection committees in my own universities and participated in similar processes across different institutions, the trend is clear—outstanding Muslim candidates are valued and embraced. It is imperative for Muslim professionals to adopt a mindset akin to that of the Jewish community—strive to become indispensable. Sir Syed Ahmed Khan, the visionary founder of AMU, envisioned a community that not only excelled but became indispensable contributors. His vision resonates in the advice to the Muslim youth: Become outstanding, and your brilliance will not go unnoticed. In a diverse and dynamic society, excellence remains the universal language of recognition and acceptance.

All this might sound preachy and boring, but hard work does not have to be boring or miserable. What made me a topper was not the number of *hours* that I put in each day, but the *quality* of study, the focus and the lack of distractions—making the hours count! Aligarh's hostel life, particularly at Aftab Hostel, was unparalleled. It was a hub of camaraderie, intellectual discussions and the inevitable gossip sessions. The limited entertainment options, primarily centred on watching movies, brought students together. Despite the lively atmosphere, my study hours did not conform to the stereotype of spending the majority of the day buried in books. Instead, a balance was struck, allocating around five to six hours, excluding classes, for academic pursuits.

An essential aspect of this balance was the unwavering commitment to attending classes. I emphasize the significance of class attendance for every student. Even if the teacher's delivery falls short, there is always something valuable to glean during those fifty minutes. Hard work, as conventionally perceived, wasn't the primary driver of my success. Instead, I attribute my academic achievements to a divine blessing, an acknowledgement that excellence is often a combination of passion and providence. My parents' blessings and prayers played a huge role in my success.

Parents' role becomes crucial to a child's success in more ways than one. I advocate for the pursuit of careers rooted in personal interests. It saddens me to witness the stress imposed by parents, echoing the sentiment expressed by our Hon'ble Prime Minister, who aptly stated that parents should not turn their child's results into a visiting card. Allowing children the freedom to choose their path fosters a genuine connection with their chosen field, often resulting in natural excellence.

Generational Dynamics: Navigating Distractions in the Digital Age

As a VC observing the current generation of law students, the infiltration of social media and smartphones raises concerns. The distractions posed by platforms like Instagram, tailored to one's likes and preferences, create a digital environment that can consume excessive time. Balancing the benefits and drawbacks of these technological advancements is crucial, ensuring that the wealth of information available does not detract from the focused pursuit of academic goals. The proliferation of distractions, particularly in the form of social media and smartphones, has become an undeniable facet of our lives. However, asserting control over students' access to these platforms is an impractical endeavour and therefore I never opt for controls.

Reflecting on my experience at NALSAR in 2012, attempts to control students' access to websites containing certain indicative words resulted in unintended consequences. Basic functionalities, such as booking train tickets, which required inputting one's gender, were affected. So much so that even the Constitution of India became inaccessible as it contained synonyms of 'gender' in provisions relating to non-discrimination, etc. The blanket nature of word filters demonstrated that we cannot control students' use of the Internet, but we can counsel them about the legitimate use of university resources. The incident highlighted the futility of restrictive measures and prompted a reconsideration of the approach to university administration.

Embracing what I term the 'liberty model' of university administration, I reject the idea of universities functioning as authoritarian entities. Instead, recognizing the intellectual prowess of Generation Z (or Gen Z) students, I advocate for leveraging their access to social media as an advantage. Consider the efficiency gains—a task that would take hours for me to accomplish through traditional means can be completed by today's students in mere minutes. These abilities should be harnessed rather than resisted. The instantaneous access to information that technology provides is unparalleled. I use a lot of YouTube videos in my classes.

However, a more profound concern arises in the realm of interpersonal dynamics. Observing families where each member is engrossed in her or his individual screen rather than engaging in face-to-face conversations raises alarms. A Chinese video depicting a mother withholding food until mobile devices are deposited serves as a stark example of the adverse impact on real-time interpersonal connections.

The risk lies in the virtual realm substituting genuine human interaction, leading to a scenario where individuals may have an abundance of Facebook friends but lack authentic, in-person connections. This shift, while emblematic of our digitized age, prompts contemplation on the potential ramifications for human civilization. As we traverse further into this era of unprecedented connectivity, the challenge lies in preserving the essence of genuine human relationships amid the ever-expanding digital landscape.

Systemic Challenges for the Muslim Community in Indian Education: A Call for Philanthropic Action

The systemic challenges faced by the Muslim community in India, particularly in education and employment, are multifaceted and demand urgent attention. Looking at the educational landscape, Muslim representation in higher education remains alarmingly low, hovering around 5 per cent[1]. While recent years have seen a positive trend among Muslim girls[2], the overall community representation is far from proportional to its population share of 14–15 per cent.

Several studies, notably those by the Justice Sachar Committee and the Professor Amitabh Kundu Committee, have underscored the educational disparities faced by Muslims. Astonishingly, the community lags behind Scheduled Castes and Scheduled Tribes, who have made strides due to constitutional provisions like reservations. Unlike Scheduled Castes and Scheduled Tribes, Muslims cannot benefit from state-sponsored reservations due to constitutional constraints.* However, the Constitution provides an alternative route for minorities to establish educational institutions of their choice. Here lies the clarion call for Muslim philanthropists to step forward and establish more educational institutions. While historical Muslim

---

* Editor's note: Muslims are eligible to avail of the EWS and OBC reservation, though.

institutions exist, some suffer from mismanagement, presenting an opportunity for a paradigm shift.

The success of Christian institutions, widely regarded as the best in various cities, serves as an inspiring model. Muslims must heavily invest in education and take charge of establishing their educational institutions, reducing dependence on the government. While it is the government's responsibility, post-Article 21A, to provide education for six to fourteen-year-olds, Muslims must seize the full advantage of the Right to Education Act, 2009, and Article 30, which gives minorities 'fundamental rights' to establish and administer educational institutions of their choice.

The government should actively encourage minority institutions, rejecting baseless claims of appeasement. Contrary to misconceptions, minority institutions are not exclusionary; they contribute significantly to the nation's fabric. Institutions like St Stephen's have a majority of non-Christian students, demonstrating the inclusive nature of such establishments.

Muslims setting up educational institutions face internal challenges, often contending with criticism and fatwas from within the community. A notable example is Sir Syed Ahmed Khan, who received various fatwas, even calling for the demolition of the college he founded![3] This internal struggle necessitates government support and recognition. Liberal Muslims are, in fact, in a battle within their own community.

To encourage the transition from madrasas to mainstream liberal education, the government should provide more grant-in-aid to minority educational institutions. This strategic investment will empower individuals with a modern, liberal, and secular education, enabling them to contribute meaningfully to the nation's progress. Any such investment basically serves the national interest. The onus is not only on the government but also on the Muslim community to join hands in this transformative educational journey.

The concern surrounding minority institutions, often viewed as potential enclaves for fostering aloofness or separatist thoughts, requires nuanced consideration. It's crucial to dispel misconceptions and differentiate these institutions from madrasas. For instance, my alma mater, AMU, and other minority institutions like Jamia Millia Islamia play a vital role in shaping a diverse educational landscape. Contrary to the fear of exclusivity, minority institutions operate on a foundation of inclusivity. These institutions, shielded by the protective umbrella of Article 30, are not meant to breed separatism. Approximately 50 per cent of students in minority institutions are non-minorities, fostering an environment that preserves cultural diversity[4]. Religious instruction, prohibited in state institutions, finds a legitimate space in these minority educational settings provided it is given with the consent of parents.

The Supreme Court has emphasized that the rights accorded to minorities under Article 30 are part of the 'basic structure of the constitution'. Therefore, discussions about minority institutions must revolve around establishing centres of modern, liberal, and secular education. Minority communities must actively contribute to education by establishing more institutions. These institutions, aligned with constitutional principles, become agents of inclusivity rather than exclusion.

In the pursuit of inclusivity, the focus turns to the policy level. The government should champion efforts to bring about a more inclusive education system. Initiatives like the Right to Education (RTE) need proper implementation, coupled with a concerted effort to address the quality of education nationally. Regional disparities, with the south outperforming the north in terms of inclusion, prompt a call for learning from successful models and implementing educational reforms that align with the constitutional ethos.

At the individual level, striving for excellence is not merely a personal pursuit but a fundamental duty of every citizen enshrined in Article 51A of the Constitution. Whether at the community or individual level, our actions should align with constitutional values. The balancing of rights and duties ensures harmony in society and contributes to the nation's overarching goal, envisioned as a Viksit Bharat by 2047.

Muslim Personal Law, Constitutional Ethos and Social Reform

Delving into the socio–economic landscape and the challenges faced by the Muslim community, it becomes imperative to scrutinize the role of the clergy in shaping discourses. Addressing systemic issues requires a recalibration of focus towards tangible initiatives that uplift the socio–economic status of the community. However, the clergy, at times, is found misleading the masses by raising non-issues.

A pivotal strategy to foster socio–economic development is to channel concerns and discussions within the constitutional framework. The emphasis must be on addressing issues that find resonance within the constitutional provisions. The principle of equality, a cornerstone of our constitutional setup, renders discriminatory laws untenable. Herein lies the crux: the clergy must align the task of interpretation with internal reforms, ensuring the removal of discriminatory provisions to align with constitutional tenets.

Take, for instance, the complex landscape of marriage and divorce within the Muslim community. A nuanced understanding reveals that aligning with Quranic principles, such as divorce by mutual consent, or *talaq-e-ehsan*, can circumvent objections. The controversy surrounding triple divorce, deemed arbitrary and unequal, prompted judicial intervention.

While the courts rightly addressed the inherent problems, a legal critique emerged.

It becomes essential to distinguish legal reasoning from theological justifications. We should not say that triple divorce is not valid because the Qur'an does not talk about it[5]. Theological arguments asserting the sinfulness of a practice shouldn't be the basis for legal validity. The jurisprudential perspective underscores that even if a practice is sanctioned by religious texts, it may contravene the principles of a modern constitutional democracy. This critique challenges prevailing norms, asserting that certain practices, even if found in religious scriptures, must not be permitted in a progressive society.

Analysing a specific Supreme Court judgment on triple divorce (Shayara Bano v. Union of India (2017) 9 SCC 1) reveals further critiques. Reading triple divorce into the Sharia Act*, though this type of divorce is not mentioned therein, the statutory interpretation raises concerns[6]. Judicial interventions should ideally align with existing legal frameworks and precedents. Moreover, the lack of clarity on the consequences of uttering triple divorce necessitates a comprehensive approach to interpreting the judgment.

This critique, grounded in legal intricacies and constitutional principles, aims to foster a more

---

* Muslim Personal Law (Shariat) Application Act, 1937.

nuanced understanding of the complex interplay between religious practices and legal frameworks. It underscores the need for comprehensive legal reasoning that respects both religious sentiments and constitutional imperatives. In navigating the legal narratives, the quest remains for a delicate balance that upholds individual freedoms within the contours of constitutional ideals.

In exploring the intricate legal landscape surrounding issues such as polygamy within the Muslim community, a broader reflection on legal codification and its implications surfaces. The absence of a comprehensive legal framework akin to the Hindu Code Bill, which codified Hindu laws, raises questions about the missed opportunities for uniformity and systemic reform, although a historical analysis of the Hindu Code Bill reveals resistance from within the Hindu community itself. Dr Ambedkar's visionary legislation faced staunch opposition, with prominent figures like the Congress president, the leader of the house, and even the President of the nation expressing dissent. This resistance led to compromises, diluting the bill and deferring certain rights for women until much later.

Globally, amending laws for the majority is more straightforward than for minority communities. The nuanced interplay between societal attitudes, legal reforms and the minority psyche underscores the challenges faced in legal amendments. A central contention emerges concerning the UCC, a constitutional principle awaiting enactment. The Muslim community, largely guided by the clergy and self-serving political leadership, has witnessed a reluctance to initiate internal law reforms. The emphasis on the community taking the lead in aligning practices with constitutional ideals and addressing issues like polygamy underscores the need for proactive measures.

The contention that Uttarakhand prohibiting polygamy is not an interference in Islam finds support in Quranic principles, emphasizing monogamy as the general rule and polygamy as a rare exception under stringent conditions. However, we should keep in mind that legal changes may not necessarily induce social reform; instead, a comprehensive approach involving education and social reform is imperative. Freedom of religion should include freedom within religion as well as freedom from religion. We must emphasize constitutional morality over excessive religiosity. The time has come to relegate religion to the private sphere and nurture a society rooted in rationality.

Legal Disputes and Pragmatic Solutions

On the issue of religious disputes, particularly in the aftermath of Ayodhya, Gyanwapi and the emerging discourse around Mathura, I must express my reservations about the legal route for resolving religious disputes, advocating instead for amicable and localized solutions that avoid nationalizing these delicate matters, in the spirit of alternative dispute resolution methods.

After the Babri Masjid's demolition, it would have been prudent for the Muslim leadership to hand over the disputed land to Hindus, thus preventing protracted legal battles. There is limited significance to the land without the mosque, and we must steer clear of extreme claims that hinder arbitration and compromise.

Drawing lessons from Ayodhya, I propose resolving disputes outside the courtroom through arbitration, fostering a process of mutual concessions. Despite the existence of numerous mosques that were built in the Mughal period, specific locations, such as Kashi and Mathura, possessing unique significance for Hindus, require a more localized and community-driven approach to dispute resolution.

Looking at the overwhelming evidence of temple destruction in Mathura, I must stress the need to avoid protracted legal battles that risk societal polarization. Navigating religious disputes requires advocating for a balance between legal considerations and pragmatic solutions to foster harmony and inter-community relations.

Conclusion

I want to conclude with a message to the Indian youth at large, especially Gen Z, which is an aspirational generation that refuses to accept sub-standard treatment and sub-par facilities. They even refuse to put up with relationships that they deem toxic. Unlike the generations preceding them, who believed in keeping up appearances, Gen Z believes in 'keeping it real'. I see cause for optimism in their sincerity and rejection of mediocrity, whether in professional life or in interpersonal relationships. Their aspirational standards and quest for excellence must be properly channelled for national development.

Article 51(A)(j) makes it the duty of every Indian citizen to strive for excellence, and I am optimistic about Gen Z's ability to fulfil this duty. This Amrit Peedhi should strive for individual excellence and contribute to societal progress, making India a developed nation by 2047, in line with the Hon'ble PM's vision for Bharat, who has clearly said that India's strength lies in its diversity. Let us all be proud of our cultural, linguistic and religious diversity. Let us work towards preserving the rich heritage of our composite culture.

Why Prime Minister Narendra Modi Is My Role Model

—Prof. Tariq Mansoor

- Prof. (Dr) Tariq Mansoor is an Indian academic and Professor of Surgery, and former VC of the AMU. With about four decades of teaching, research, clinical and administrative experience, he has 115 publications to his credit and has supervised theses of 58 postgraduate medical students. Earlier, he also served as Principal and Chief Medical Superintendent as well as Chairman, Department of Surgery at J.N. Medical College and Hospital, AMU, the largest teaching and tertiary medical care centre in western UP.
- He is presently a member of the UP Legislative Council and national vice-president of the Bharatiya Janata Party.

- During his term as VC, AMU was accredited A+ Grade by NAAC and was among five Central Universities granted Category II Autonomy by University Grants Commission. As VC of AMU, he introduced numerous cutting-edge courses and established the College of Nursing, Para Medical College, Department of Cardiology and Centres for Bio Medical Engineering, AI, Green & Renewable Energy, Dara Shikoh Centre of Interfaith Understanding and Dialogue, etc., and obtained statutory approval for Institute of Pharmacy from the President of India.

- A keen tennis player, he has reading interests in education, history, international affairs, and politics. His opinion pieces on a wide range of issues are often carried by leading dailies.

I am a teacher, a doctor and a people's representative in that order. I belong to a family of academicians. My late father, Prof. Hafeezul Rahman, was the founder dean of the faculty of law at AMU. From a very young age, I developed a habit of reading books and newspapers. My favourite newspaper was The *Statesman*, which was the most widely circulated English newspaper in north India at the time and well-known for its editorial page. Reputed faculty of AMU as well as from other parts of India were regular visitors to our residence, and I would interact with them and observe them as they conversed. There was never a dearth of role models.

Parents and family are always important in shaping you, both as a person and as a professional. They shape your values and aspirations. I was raised in a joint family and values like loyalty and commitment were instilled in me from the beginning. My eldest brother, the late Prof. Rasheeduzzafar (former VC, Jamia Hamdard University) played a significant role in shaping my aspirations, as I looked up to him. My cosmopolitan education at a Christian missionary school (Our Lady of Fatima, Aligarh) also taught me lessons in discipline, punctuality, harmony and teamwork. My parents, especially my mother, motivated me to pursue a career in medicine. She also encouraged me to take up surgery. Who I am as a person and as a professional is therefore a product of these many influences.

Had I not been selected in medicine, I may have pursued a career in either history or law. Even today, I am fascinated by history. However, my mother's prayers prevailed and I got into the MBBS course at J.N. Medical College, AMU, in my very first attempt. This key moment defined the rest of my career trajectory. My selection as a teaching faculty member in the Department of Surgery at AMU was another important milestone. Later, I developed an interest in breast and thyroid diseases and tried to give my best to both my patients and my students. Making a difference in the lives of others motivated me then, as it motivates me now. I have always strived to provide excellence in teaching and affordable health care to patients. I tell my students that if you want to be a good professional, you must first be a good human being.

I would advise the youth of today to pursue their field of interest and be passionate about it. Only when each of us contributes our best to our respective fields can we become a developed nation by 2047. We should be cognizant of the global competition and work to strengthen our nation, not wasting crucial years of youth in frivolous pursuits. Youth should take up co-curricular and extra-curricular activities such as sports, debates, cultural activities, etc., in the right earnest and should have a positive and optimistic attitude towards life. You should have short-term and long-term career goals. Young people should dream big and be ambitious in life. Despite a shortage of time, I decided to lend my voice to this book, as it is important for youth to have role models whom they can look up to and relate to.

People have different role models and influences at various stages of life. Parents, teachers, friends and colleagues have variously been important influences at various stages of my life and career. I have also held leadership positions in my academic life. I was elected president of the Association of Surgeons of India (UP), secretary of the AMU Teachers' Association and three times a member of the executive council of AMU, representing the teaching faculty. Communication skills are key to success in the fields of medicine and academia, and I had an edge in these areas, which helped me in my leadership roles as well.

The most important qualities for leadership are common sense and the ability to learn from mistakes. If you commit a mistake, the first priority should be to rectify it if possible and not to repeat it. Dialogue and consultations are important in any leadership role, especially in academic institutions. Leadership must be decisive but devoid of ego. Today, as I have embarked upon a new leadership role after a long and fulfilling academic and administrative career, I see Prime Minister Narendra Modi as a role model for his leadership qualities, hard work, communication skills and commitment towards national development and progress.

Prime Minister Narendra Modi has sought to redefine welfarism as a political duty covering a wide spectrum of human needs—food, housing, sanitation, gas, water and healthcare. The Pradhan Mantri Garib Kalyan Yojana (PMGKY)—the largest welfare scheme in history—fed 810 million Indians during the existential crisis of the pandemic.[1] No home was left out because of the name on the door! Drawing from the success of the scheme, it was extended beyond the pandemic as Pradhan Mantri Garib Kalyan Anna Yojana (PMGKAY) for a period of five years.[2] It benefits all communities, irrespective of faith.

Further, the introduction of the PM Vishwakarma scheme will give a fillip to socially disadvantaged group-led enterprises and artisans such as tailors, barbers, weavers, etc., carving out a specific category of labharthis* within the economically marginalized Pasmandas. Even though the scheme is not specific to Muslims, the eighteen crafts listed under the scheme mirror the occupational profiles of a large number of backward-caste Muslims engaged in these trades. All this underscores a truly inclusive vision of development, which I endeavour to emulate in my leadership style.

Prime Minister Narendra Modi has been repeatedly invoking issues of social justice to address anomalies within the Muslim community. The Pasmandas—a social sub-group representing the most backward and underprivileged Muslims, constituting roughly 80 per cent of the Indian Muslim population[3]—form the core of this strategy. His willingness to accommodate the Pasmandas offers a promise of ending the hegemony of elites. By making calls for greater democratization and inclusivity, he seeks to address the key Pasmanda demand not to view Muslims monolithically but rather heterogeneously like other communities.

Not only does it mark the first official attempt to co-opt Muslims, but it is also the first in Indian politics where the Pasmandas—the bulk of the Muslim population—have been brought to the centre stage. Second, Modi ji has prioritized issues of gender justice in certain community personal laws. The

* The term 'labharthis' refers to beneficiaries of welfare schemes.

abolishment of the archaic practice of instant triple talaq, which incidentally is not prevalent even in the Gulf nations, has found resounding support amongst Muslim women, especially the underprivileged, who are kept in constant fear in the name of talaq. Information technology and various government schemes, both at the Centre and state levels, have played a significant role in positively impacting the educational and professional opportunities for the Muslim community.

Despite all this, the percentage of enrolment of Muslim students in schools and universities is lower than that of other socio–economically weaker sections. To rectify this, more awareness and efforts are needed, especially in promoting girl education. Muslims should send their children to school, and youth should avail of reservations under the non-discriminatory EWS (economically weaker sections) reservation brought in by the government.

It is important for us to come out of victimhood narratives and lip service rendered to us for decades by politicians and follow a statesman like Prime Minister Narendra Modi not necessarily in a political sense but at a personal level: he is grounded, and he embodies sacrifice, hard work, fitness, impartiality, secularism, vision, humility, professional excellence, mental resilience, authenticity and selflessness. We should emulate his values in order to succeed professionally in our lives.

No doubt, we Muslims have always been proud Indians. But now is the time to be especially proud, given the vast strides that India is making on the global stage under Prime Minister Narendra Modi's visionary leadership. Earlier, we would argue that we were better off compared to Pakistan or Bangladesh. Today, we compare ourselves to developed western nations in terms of outer space exploration, vaccine coverage, national income, ease of living, ease of commute, ease of doing business and commitment to sustainability.

Today, the Indian passport evokes respect abroad like never before. You see it in the intangible things, like the behaviour of the immigration officers towards you, but you also see it in the tangible impacts, such as Italy's exit from the Belt and Road Initiative (BRI), which is a major strategic victory for India. Our engagement with OIC (Organisation of Islamic Cooperation) nations has gained unprecedented momentum and this has led to real outcomes such as the royal pardon and homecoming of the Indian Navy veterans who were on death row in Qatar or the efforts towards settling trade in Rupees with the UAE.

By enabling a vibrant FinTech and startup environment, the Government of India has created the conditions for entrepreneurs to solve problems ranging from the smallest to the biggest. Sure, one can say that gig work-based platforms were made possible by technological advances, which were anyway inevitable, and one may also argue that they are successful due to the large availability of cheap semi-skilled labour in India, but it is only under Prime Minister Narendra Modi's leadership that India's demographic 'problems' have been turned into a demographic advantage and that the business environment needed for startups that could engage this demographic has been enabled. I frequently travel abroad, and I can confidently say that the ease of living in India is unmatched at present, due to the coming together of our technological and demographic strengths.

To Muslim youth and to Indian youth in general, I would like to say that India is a truly secular nation where one can overcome most hurdles through hard work and by being the best in one's field. This means that you will still have to face hardship, but who doesn't have to struggle? Nobody in this country has it easy, given the sheer size of our population and the competition. But we need to maintain a positive mindset. Not only that, but we also need to upskill ourselves on a regular basis to stay relevant in our fields. This is true of every single field, including the Army, IAS, IPS, etc.

Never think that you will crack one exam, and then life will be a bed of roses. People in all walks of life are grappling with new changes such as AI, social media, etc. Think of my generation's encounter with email, touchscreens, plagiarism detection software, social media, etc.—was it a smooth transition? No. But we do what we need to do to keep up. This is the reality of professional life. It is a process of constant self-improvement, but it is also rewarding. Also, at times, we simply fail, and that's okay. That's just life. But it is only through constant trial and error, combined with patience and self-improvement, that we can become the best version of ourselves while also making a Viksit Bharat by 2047, Inshallah!

For the Love of the Land

—Asif Bhamla

- Asif Bhamla is an environmentalist and founder of the Bhamla Foundation, which uses popular messaging to encourage people to take responsibility for cleaning up beaches and keeping public spaces clean, besides making small, sustainable lifestyle choices on a daily basis.
- He was awarded the National Green Crusader by the Government of India and the United Nations Environment Programme. Asif and his daughter, Saher Bhamla, are global advocates for sustainable living.
- The Bhamla Foundation's campaign 'Tik Tik Plastic' mobilized the Hindi film industry's star power to discourage the use of single-use plastics. The viral hit even made an appearance at the UN headquarters in New York.

- The Bhamla Foundation has over 18,000 'eco-champs' across India that pioneer voluntary activities such as cleaning up public spaces, waste management initiatives, promoting sustainable living through recycling and green commute, etc. More recently, the Bhamla Foundation launched the Bhoomi Namaskar campaign, which was also a huge success
- He is a spokesperson for the Bharatiya Janata Party.

The invitation to contribute a chapter to this book was accompanied by the brief that it is a book about Indian Muslim achievers and role models. So it entailed speaking about my work as an Indian and as a Muslim. What can I say as an Indian Muslim, except that I am incredibly fortunate to have been born in this land and that it is my love for this land—literally and figuratively—that drives me to do what I do? We are grateful to our ancestors for choosing India over Pakistan. There is a public square named after my father, the Haji Vali Mohammad Bhamla Chowk in Bandra, in the financial capital of India, in the heart of where Bollywood lives! But this is not what we were told by advocates of the two-nation theory, were we? We were told that we would not be safe in India, but we have excelled in every field that you can possibly name. And this book is a testament to that.

I began my activism during my college days with an initiative called 'I Love Bandra', organizing cleaning drives and awareness campaigns on littering, waste disposal and other civic issues. However, it soon gained momentum, echoing the concerns of numerous other Mumbaikars and someone suggested that I give it a broader name that could include campaigns outside of Bandra. Thus, the Bhamla Foundation was born. Mumbai's pollution issue needs no elaboration. One of the biggest metropolises in India, it is full of domestic waste and industrial effluents that eventually find their way into the sea. It is also home to one of the biggest slums in Asia, creating unsanitary conditions for millions of people. The Bhamla Foundation raised these issues by promoting cleanliness, educating people about the correct way of disposing of garbage, recycling, composting, etc. Our slogan was 'Clean Mumbai, Green Mumbai'.

We always understood that we are a drop in the ocean, but it is the drops that make the ocean! The Bhamla Foundation is my life's work, and I have been fortunate to have had the support of celebrities from the Hindi film industry, sports, politics and so on. Long before the social media 'influencer' culture, we understood that cleanliness and sustainability require deep cultural change that celebrities are best placed to initiate. Hence, I have never shied away from mobilizing star power for a good cause. Our song, 'Tik Tik Plastic', which mobilized Bollywood top stars to talk about single-use plastics, embodied the spirit of making sustainability and cleanliness cool.

However, 2 October 2014 was a game-changer for organizations like ours when Prime Minister Narendra Modi launched the Swachh Bharat Abhiyan (Clean India campaign). Our team was overjoyed when Prime Minister Narendra Modi decided to use his voice for a cause that the father of our nation had envisioned, reclaiming a side of Gandhi that had been conveniently overlooked thus far, because who wants to talk about cleanliness, right? As a topic, it is not controversial enough, not trendy enough, not glamorous enough and not populist enough.

People dislike being sermonized about cleanliness, wastefulness, littering, proper waste disposal, etc. During the twenty-seven years of our work, we have tried our best not to be preachy about cleanliness. And the genius of the Swachh Bharat campaign lay in the fact that the PM himself held a broom. Cynics made fun of the act, just as they have made fun of us all these years, but we knew full well what kind of deep cultural impact he was trying to make. His act immediately lifted the spirits of countless *safai karamcharis* (janitors) across the country, who are our biggest allies in the goal of making India clean and green. It boosted their morale, giving dignity to their work.

One important aspect of Swachh Bharat is that it has given visibility and dignity to women's work, as the primary responsibility of cleanliness in our society falls upon women's shoulders. The construction of over ten crore toilets under Swachh Bharat has also ensured women's safety, as open defecation renders women vulnerable to harassment and other forms of danger[1].

It is no secret that we, Indians, are a messy lot, but some people extrapolate 'what is' and argue that nothing can ever change. Change can happen if those with influence use their voices for the right causes. No leader before Prime Minister Narendra Modi had tried to educate the electorate about the need to get our act together and take responsibility for cleaning our surroundings. An interesting observation often made by foreigners visiting India is that while we keep our homes clean, we tend to litter the outdoors, a classic tragedy of the commons. Why are we like this? Because no one has taught us otherwise. In a democracy, politicians often feel compelled to treat their electorate with kid gloves, not spelling out the bitter truth, in what is known as 'appeasement'. Typically, politicians raise 'people's issues'—issues that people consider important. Very few leaders have the strength to speak the truth to the people. Prime Minister Narendra Modi proved himself a visionary by highlighting an issue that people need to be educated about.

Conversely, Prime Minister Narendra Modi has also summoned Bharat's civilizational strengths and our original way of life, marked by austerity, conservationism, saving, mindfulness and thoughtful consumption, reminding us of who we really are! Unfortunately, wastefulness, consumerism, and extravagance are perils of modern urban life, especially in the twenty-first century, whereas our indigenous traditions of sustainability, frugality, and reuse can be resurrected to promote a circular economy. This is the essence of 'Lifestyle for the Environment' (or LiFE), a concept that India is trying to promote globally in various ways. One of the pillars of yoga is mindfulness and by promoting yoga globally, Prime Minister Narendra Modi is also indirectly promoting mindfulness, something that the Bhamla Foundation promotes by asking people to consume mindfully.

We do not and should not expect perfection from people. Shaming people for using plastics may not be effective and being hypercritical damages the cause in the same way that fundamentalism does damage to faith. Environmentalism entails that we do our best. Even if all of us only did our best, we would be better off. The promotion of sustainable crops, such as millets, across the world by India under Prime Minister Narendra Modi, is also an aspect of our traditional strengths being summoned to provide a way forward to the world in what is going to be an increasingly drought-prone future.

Speaking of indigenous traditions, I would say that there is a misconception that Islam is an anthropocentric religion, because Islam calls for moderation and for limiting desires[2]. There are a number of Hadiths that stress the importance of planting trees.[3] He pioneered the concept of protected areas (*hima* and *haram*) where natural resources would not be used for certain periods of time, promoting conservation of resources and allowing them to replenish themselves.[4] The Prophet (PBUH) clearly warned his followers to show discernment and avoid felling trees even during war. As Muslims, we too have a responsibility towards nature.

For me, it's simple: I love my daughters more than anything else in the world. So, I ask myself every day: if my father handed down a habitable world to me, what kind of planet am I leaving behind for my daughters, and for their subsequent generations? If we asked ourselves this simple question on a daily basis, we would find enough motivation for our sustainable actions. I find true joy in knowing that my extremely talented daughter, Saher Bhamla, has found my cause worthy and joined me in it from a very young age. Together, we attended the COP-28 in Dubai, and our chests swelled with pride to see the respect that India commands at global forums today. Everywhere we go, we are asked where we are from, and when we say, 'India', people reply, 'Oh, Modi's India?'

The Bhamla Foundation has been representing Indian civil society at the UN and other global forums for decades, but Prime Minister Narendra Modi's global outlook and his environmentalism with *jan bhagidari* (grassroots participation) are altogether different from other top-down governmental approaches. He deserves credit for using his voice to inculcate good values at the grassroots through programmes like the *Mann Ki Baat* radio show. This has inspired idealistic youth in all parts of the country to take up the cause, such as the seven-year-old girl, Jannat, from Kashmir, who found a mention in the PM's *Mann Ki Baat* show for running cleanliness drives in Kashmir's Dal Lake. While many of the people of my age have accepted our filthy surroundings as fait accompli, as something that cannot be changed, it is the idealism of the youth that we can count on. I see hope in youngsters like Saher and Jannat, who will take the cause forward and inspire more people to join the movement.

Ten or fifteen years ago, when the Bhamla Foundation would celebrate World Environment Day or Earth Day, people did not understand the importance of these observances. However, today, with extreme climate events becoming routine, the world has woken up to the devastating impacts of climate change. We are fortunate that while many world leaders are climate change deniers, Prime Minister Narendra Modi is a highly intelligent statesman who understands the importance of this issue and who has a scientific approach to environmental issues. His climate advocacy can save our planet from doom, as it exerts pressure on other world leaders to take climate change seriously. India is heading in the right direction by aiming to increase the proportion of solar power in its energy basket while not compromising on our growth and development.

Diplomacy in the future will require more emphasis on climate diplomacy and sustainability, and India is preparing itself for the future by embarking upon a mission to develop smart cities and by developing and showcasing sustainable solutions using the latest technologies, such as IoT (Internet of Things) devices and the like. Climate-smart agriculture, smart irrigation, etc. are massive tasks, but at least now we have started our journey towards that. Prime Minister Narendra Modi's environmentalism provides an umbrella for our orphan efforts towards cleanliness, so we see him as a guardian. The PM's appeal cuts across communities, regions and genders and, dare I say, countries. His voice truly matters to us as environmentalists.

I champion the cause of cleanliness so that more foreign tourists can visit Mumbai, contributing to our GDP, but a single terror attack can set all the progress back, leading to travel advisories by various nations instead. As a Mumbaikar, I was shocked and petrified when the 26/11 terror attacks turned the financial capital of India into the capital of fear. It was a rude awakening for India that Pakistan could strike terror in the heart of what is considered one of the safest cities in India, our Mumbai!

As a Mumbaikar traumatized by the 26/11 attacks, I am grateful to Prime Minister Narendra Modi for taking strong measures against Pakistan, such as the 2016 surgical strikes in Uri, the 2019 Balakot air strike, the diplomatic measures, the abrogation of Article 370 and last but not least, the deep connection that Prime Minister Narendra Modi and Home Minister Amit Shah have established with the people of Jammu & Kashmir, winning their hearts and providing them security and an atmosphere to fearlessly express themselves.

As a nation that used to cower in fear of aggression from the other side, the Modi government has a strong message that India will no longer suffer in silence and will retaliate if provoked. This has brought a sense of relief to every Indian. The 1990s and 2000s used to be a time when bomb blasts had become routine, terror attacks had created a perennial atmosphere of 'red alert' at every market, every festival and so on.[5] Anyone who has lived through that time can tell the difference between then and now. As per the South Asia Terrorism Portal (SATP), the number of terrorist incidents has come down from 3,022 in the year 2000 to 886 in 2024.[6] I am well aware of the devastating impacts that a single terror attack or even a bomb scare can have on a business establishment. Hence, I have no hesitation in expressing myself freely about how Prime Minister Narendra Modi's leadership has been a blessing for us.

It is important to note that Muslims are not single-issue voters. We care about climate change and environmental issues just as much as anyone else. I hope that this book succeeds in showcasing the diversity of contributions that Muslims make to public life in India, from which Muslim youth and, in general, Indian youth can derive inspiration and develop themselves professionally. I have done whatever I have done for the love of the land, for my *sarzameen*, and that spirit should be enough to drive us to be the best version of ourselves and contribute towards building a Viksit Bharat by 2047.

Change Doesn't Stop Because a Theory Says It Is Impossible

—Shehla Rashid

- Shehla Rashid is a policy consultant, researcher and academic with research interests in science and technology studies (STS), a field of social science that examines the relationship between scientific knowledge, technological systems and society.
- She has distinguished herself academically, earning the coveted UGC-NET/JRF fellowship in sociology in 2014 and again in 2023, emerging as a Jammu & Kashmir-level topper in a recruitment exam held for an assistant professorship in social science.
- She also topped the JNU Entrance Examination (JNUEE) in 2015 for an integrated MPhil-PhD

programme in Law & Governance (an offshoot of political science).

- She has worked on research projects at Microsoft Research India and is regularly consulted by various tech companies, including the top five on cultural aspects of the development of AI-based tools, Generative AI models, social media design and the critical evaluation of technological products and systems.

- She was elected the vice president of the Jawaharlal Nehru University Students' Union (JNUSU) in 2015, making her the first Kashmiri woman office-bearer of the JNUSU. She secured the highest number of votes polled that year for any post in the students' union.

- She is one of the most well-known youth faces in India in the field of politics and activism, as she has led various successful student movements which have been the subject of an ill-fated web series and a movie.[1] She is the first non-dynast woman from Kashmir to have made a name for herself in Indian politics.

- An advocate for women's mental health, she started the conversation on lesser-known issues like PMDD (pre-menstrual dysphoric disorder) in India.

- She is also consulted by companies wishing to implement inclusive workplace policies.

- A passionate hiker, she advocates for keeping mountain trails litter free.
- If you are reading this in print, then she is also a published author by now.

You probably remember me as the first Kashmiri woman to be elected as an office-bearer of the Jawaharlal Nehru University Students' Union in 2015. You may remember that I led and ably steered a powerful students' movement or my interventions at the India Today Conclave in 2016 on Kashmir, whose viewership ran into tens of millions. Or you may remember me as the general secretary of a newly launched political party in Jammu & Kashmir, which was dissolved before it could be registered!

You could also be one of my million odd followers on social media or you may recall my more recent podcast on ANI, where I acknowledged the massive improvement in the security situation, a better human rights record and peace and development in Jammu & Kashmir after the removal of Article 370, which was also watched millions of times across platforms. This essay is a brief story of where I come from, the questions that I struggled with and what led me to re-examine my strongly-held political views.

It's also possible that you don't know me at all and that your introduction to me is through this book, which is the first-of-its-kind in India. Despite my overtly political credentials, I have never held membership of a registered political party. Yet, I hold the most important political office in the country—that of a *citizen*.

I grew up in Downtown, Srinagar, in a locality called Sona Masjid, Habba Kadal, very close to the Raghunath temple by the river Jhelum. Downtown, Srinagar can be accurately described as the epicentre of the insurgency of the late 1980s and early 1990s that eventually led to the exodus of Kashmiri Pandits from the Valley. I had a disturbed childhood by virtue of growing up in a broken home in a conflict zone, but I found refuge in books. I could get lost in the world of science and literature for hours at a stretch—it was a form of escape.

I would read the theory section in mathematics textbooks, study the Oxford English Dictionary to build my vocabulary, finish off a semester-long reading list in a few weeks, and even study the books of higher classes in advance. I read the history of the slave trade in detail in sixth grade and devoured encyclopedias such as the *Tell Me Why* series. I finished reading my mother's big fat book on human psychology by the seventh standard, and so on. She would get me magazines such as *Reader's Digest*, *Wisdom*, *Competition Success Review*, *Malayala Manorama*, etc. I would routinely top state-level talent search examinations, giving me confidence in myself. But my curiosity was insatiable, so my mother would at times deposit me for the day in the massive library at the Sher-e-Kashmir Institute of

Medical Sciences (SKIMS) where she worked and let me read more advanced books and encyclopedias on her account.

Finding escape in the world of books made sense. It gave me more than an escape—it gave me an academic edge, which is the real 'escape' from reality, because academic advancement lets us become whoever we want, unshackled from the limitations of where we come from. Academic excellence, especially in a knowledge economy like India, is our best ticket to a life away from poverty, conflict, etc. Even our political views are better received when we distinguish ourselves academically.

I went to some of the premier educational institutions in India, wrote various reports and papers, earned several degrees and fellowships and worked in cutting-edge areas at the intersection of technology and politics, visiting various countries. While doing all this, I also managed to make my mark politically in a country of over a billion people, even though I may not know to what effect just yet, raising important issues while maintaining a rational take on things, adding value to my craft and never doing anything half-heartedly.

We can differentiate ourselves in any field by adding value to our work—be it voluntary work (such as activism) or profitable work—and we can do so by bringing fresh insights and methods to it. We must strive to be the best at whatever we choose to do. Don't be modest in what you aspire for, and don't be orthodox. Bringing your prior knowledge and diverse experiences to a craft is something that you shouldn't shy away from. I have formally studied engineering, public policy, sociology, political science and philosophy in that order. I do not see knowledge in silos.

Before philosophy and mathematics became separate branches of knowledge, they were one and the same. Well-known French philosopher René Descartes[2] of 'Cogito ergo sum' fame, who is often known as the 'Father of Modern Philosophy', also gave us the system of Cartesian coordinates, which is named after him and which forms the basis of analytic geometry[3]. Similarly, religious reflection and metaphysical inquiry permeated early physics, and Sir Isaac Newton constantly strove to reconcile his scientific observations with his religious beliefs[4]. There is no harm in drawing knowledge from various fields—inspiration is all around us, and it can come from anywhere.

Our knowledge can guide our activism. Conversely, activism can inform our academic work. I brought the entirety of my knowledge, including my tech skills, and, not least, common sense, to my activism, differentiating myself as an activist. My story also involves emerging stronger from every struggle or failure. For me, it has often involved stepping back and analysing the problem from a larger perspective. For example, despite being a gifted student, I struggled with mathematics in the fourth standard, unable to understand the logic behind long division, and got especially confused when algebra was introduced in sixth grade.

However, I refused to simply memorize problem-solving techniques to pass the exam, as I didn't believe in studying for the sake of exams. Instead, I decided to get to the bottom of the matter to understand why x and x get squared when multiplied but doubled when added, why x^2 can't be added to 2x and so on. I went to several teachers in my city, seeking answers like a monk. I faced my biggest challenge head-on and understood the logic underlying algebra instead of simply learning how to solve equations.

I continued to engage deeper, making efforts to understand the logical underpinnings of every new mathematical paradigm introduced in higher classes, such as the real-world and philosophical significance of irrational numbers, the history of trigonometry, etc. Solving problems was a cakewalk afterwards, though it still took practice. I would solve ten to fifteen mathematics problems daily. Over time, mathematics became my favourite subject, and I became the favourite student of mathematics teachers. I similarly struggled to grasp the abstractions of chemistry and take them at face value. Hence, I spent hours in libraries studying complex books on chemistry, trying to grasp things in as much depth as possible, differentiating proven phenomena from theoretical constructs.

In physics, I found vectors challenging for a few days and made efforts to grasp this topic in so much depth that my physics teacher Prof. Nazir Tantray named me 'vector girl'—it's how he remembers me even today! Easily the best physics teacher out there, he would encourage us to 'get the feel of physics,' demonstrating complex phenomena in a way that you could picture electromagnetic wave propagation and quantum phenomena in vivid three-dimensional detail. I would go much beyond what is taught in the class and solve both H.C. Verma problems as well as MCQs from QuAn banks. When the twelfth grade board examination results were announced, I was among the state-level toppers in mathematics and chemistry.

No marks for guessing, I got into engineering college and graduated with a BTech in computer science and engineering from the National Institute of Technology, Srinagar, in 2011. During the three summers of discontent—2008, 2009 and 2010—which coincided with my college years, I was awoken to the troubled history and politics of Kashmir, which affected me to the extent that I could not find purpose in my chosen stream any longer.

Though I had found campus placement in the company of my choice, my job did not offer answers to what was troubling me. At this point, I was writing code for iOS apps in a language called C# (read: C sharp), which is an object-oriented language built over C++. While I was doing well, I was troubled by more political questions and had started writing regularly on human rights issues.

I was also impacted by issues of violence against women, but I perceived a lack of theoretical understanding of gender, my understanding being limited to my own experience. I wanted to study social sciences formally but didn't have any exposure to the arts streams, as there was nobody in our family with an arts or humanities background. I didn't even know that colleges like Lady Shri Ram and Miranda House existed. So, I started looking for development sector jobs on DevNet, Times Ascent, etc.

One fine day, while surfing Times Ascent, I found an advertisement for an executive course in political leadership for women at IIM Bangalore's Centre for Public Policy. At some level, it appealed to me because, in retrospect, I feel that, deep within, I knew that this was the path I envisioned for myself. I applied and got in, and I was the youngest in the batch. It was a unique course, and it was never offered again, as Prof. Rajeev Gowda, who was then heading the centre, retired and was nominated to the Rajya Sabha. But it became a sort of bridge course for me to get into the social sciences proper.

For my master's degree, I got into sociology, standing sixth in the JNU entrance examination. Funnily, I started checking the selection list for sociology from the bottom upwards and couldn't find my name, disappointed midway along the long list of seventy names, not expecting my name to figure even in the top thirty-five and not bothering to check the list downwards from the top, as I was an engineer by education. But when I hesitantly checked the list from the top, I found myself in the sixth spot, much to my own surprise!

However, keeping up wasn't easy; sociology is somewhat German and somewhat French (verstehen, gesellschaft, gemeinschaft, zeitgeist, bourgeoise, proletariat, anomie, etc.). But I studied so hard that I ended up cracking the UGC-NET/JRF (Junior Research Fellowship) exam in my first attempt, while I was still in the second semester of my MA, whereas most people typically struggle to even crack the NET bracket despite several attempts.

While my classmates were keen on checking the NET-JRF result, I was reluctant to check mine because I wasn't expecting anything. Then a classmate took my roll number and checked my results, informing me that I had cracked JRF! I thought that it was a joke. They thought I was either being pretentious or secretive, as 'topper types' often are.

My story often involves me highly underestimating myself and then working so hard to overcompensate that I surpass all expectations, especially my own. While most of my classmates were from an arts background, I felt that I had to work much harder and ended up surpassing everyone. But my affinity for hard work isn't limited to academics. I brought my work ethic to my activism too. At JNU, I was among the most hardworking activists. I knew most students by first name, and I was as serious about my activism as I was about my studies. I poured my heart and soul into my activism and it showed.

I had made a brief foray into Kashmir politics in 2018-2019 which came to an end when the Government of India abrogated Article 370 which had given a special status to Jammu & Kashmir, after which I felt that I no longer had a theory of change and that I needed to go back to the drawing board. A knee injury following the abrogation also kept me confined for a prolonged duration of time, and this was followed by the Covid-19 lockdown. All this finally allowed me to take a much-needed break from activism, to recuperate and to simply take stock of my potential and my abilities.

I spent years locked up in a room, studying everything from genetics to philosophy to world history to government policy to frontier technologies, filling the perceived knowledge gaps that years of dedicated activism work had caused. It also meant reading more holistically, outside the knowledge that permeates to us through our filter bubbles. I went into a deep process of self-discovery to realize that I exhibit what is known as 'trait polymathy'—having interest in diverse areas of knowledge. This led me to try my hand at various competitive exams, including the civil services exam, that I thought may be a good fit for my mental make-up and commensurate with my qualifications.

Though I cracked the preliminary exam twice, I never really got the hang of mains answer writing. It's not that I didn't try hard enough—after all, I never do anything half-heartedly. My hands became calloused from answer writing practice, but some things simply aren't a fit due to how we are wired or groomed. But I believed in myself and in God. I simply allowed myself to be a young person who is in the process of self-discovery. If a certain path didn't work out, maybe it was not meant to be. For each story of success, there are numerous instances of failure that we do not hear about. This process prepared me for success in a different exam though.

I had taken up sociology and political science as optionals, enrolling at some of the top coaching academies, starting revision from scratch and putting in about sixteen to eighteen hours of study daily. This may sound cumbersome, but it was a privilege and a luxury to be able to take a break and just read whatever I wanted to read but had not been able to, because of relentless activism. It was like going back to my childhood, when I would devour books. This time, I ended up topping the recruitment exam for an assistant professorship in sociology. It was my self-doubt that became the fuel for my success.

My story of becoming a student leader has a similar theme. Though I lost the first university-level election that I contested in 2014, I can confidently say that failure teaches us more than success ever can. I went after the reasons for failure, both personal and organizational, and I invested so much energy into rectifying them, building myself and my organization in the process, that when I was elected to the students' union in 2015, I was the highest polled candidate that year for any post in the students' body, even though it was the most difficult election that our organization had faced in years. I had spent hours listening to everyone's feedback and I had been one of the most hardworking campaigners, bringing fresh energy into my activism.

Exposure to left-wing politics at the university provided answers to some troubling political questions, especially women's issues. Marxism is the first theory to systematically analyse the issue of women's domestic labour (or 'reproductive labour'), forming the basis for feminism. I was fascinated by the student leaders, taking an interest in their speeches while also focusing on my studies. I engaged in political processes such as university general body meetings (GBMs), observed the political stances of JNUSU election candidates and took an interest in campus issues as well as the societal issues raised by student leaders of the left groups.

While student activism as a formative experience makes you sharp, perceptive and extremely well-informed, it is premised on a theory of change that is confrontational, as it is often rooted in conflict theory. Conflict theory may hold all the analytical power, yet it may or may not be a template for change. We can accept the analysis while choosing a different theory of change. And I can say that I'm in a reasonably solid position to discard confrontational theories of change because I have tried them out thoroughly, and I have met people who have been trying them out for decades without much impact.

To elaborate, there are two kinds of theoretical frameworks to explain the world—conflict theories and functionalist analyses. Conflict theories such as Marxism, feminism, critical race theory (CRT), etc. see the world in the binaries of 'oppressor' and 'oppressed', actively seeking to change the status quo. Functionalist theories, on the other hand, insist on harmony, interdependence, role differentiation, etc. Functionalist theories generally uphold the status quo as a means to attaining social progress. I was naturally attracted to conflict theory, as it explained the world to me in a way that related to my formative experiences. Most university students are naturally attracted to conflict theory, as it proposes ideas of freedom, idealism and revolutionary change.

The appeal of conflict theories is difficult to put into words. Brazilian philosopher Paulo Freire wrote in his famous book, *Pedagogy of the Oppressed*, that there can be no 'oppressor' or 'oppressed' without prior violence—that the very existence of oppressor and oppressed classes is a testament to the fact that there exists violence. So, the 'oppressors' are violent by definition and cannot be called non-violent even in the absence of visible aggression. Meanwhile, the uprisings of the 'oppressed' cannot be called violent because the very fact of their oppression is premised on violence.[5] Once you read this, a whole new neural circuitry and a new way of thinking open up.

Similarly powerful is the *Manifesto of the Communist Party*, written by Karl Marx and Friedrich Engels, which, once read, can't be unread! The romance and analytical power of conflict theory are things that functionalist theories will perhaps never attain. However, the romance also arises from the fact that conflict theory tends to over-simplify matters, seeing the world in binaries and ignoring shades of grey, not bothered with unromantic detail, not accounting for individual human effort and agency, negotiation, defiance, multiplicity of identities and most importantly, multiplicity of classes. Marxism often fails to grasp the fact that there is a symbiotic relationship between the employer (capitalist) and the employed (worker) in practical life. Their interests are interwoven in the process of production; hence, there isn't a strong case for the proletariat (workers) to overthrow the establishment.

Marxism would also have you believe that there are only two classes in society—the rich and the poor—whose interests lie at polar extremes, and hence they are natural enemies. It glosses over the fact that economic gradation in society is continuous, not discrete or binary. Where you end up is a complex function of various factors such as education, skills, work ethic, luck, geography, mental resilience, culture, psychology and so on. Family heritage alone doesn't matter, as it takes knowledge, skills, ability and leadership qualities to make something of your luck. We have seen scions of prominent families being inept just as often as we have seen people without means making it big in life, especially in open societies. People with disabilities often end up defying physical, mental, societal, financial and emotional constraints to achieve great things in life.

Individual effort and human agency allow us to break out of the complex function of factors for success, and Marxist determinism doesn't account for this. Therefore, it fails to explain or predict social change, providing only for an eventual socialist revolution in vague terms. Marxism also omits mention of social mobility, progress, self-belief, individual effort and all things that actually lead to success in life, keeping you mentally trapped in a notion of inability and impossibility, even about the very basic factors for success. Hence the cliché 'if you are not a leftist in your twenties, you have no heart; but if you continue to be a leftist in your thirties, then you have no brain' and its variants. We need both our hearts and minds in the right place to make a difference, and not hearts alone.

Theories need to have three kinds of power: analytical, explanatory and predictive. While the analytical power of conflict theories such as Marxism is difficult to deny—Marx being one of the most influential philosophers of the nineteenth century—

it may not necessarily be able to explain why, for example, a newborn country like India chose to give voting rights to the entirety of her illiterate and impoverished masses (the 'proletariat') from the word go.

Similarly, while feminism is right about the existence of power dynamics in familial relations, it can't explain why women in India haven't waited for a feminist 'revolution' overthrowing the institutions of family and marriage to forge their own path to success and independence. Women who were never introduced to conflict theory have succeeded too, and their successes can be attributed to ambition and individual effort.

That is what is meant by having or lacking explanatory power. While conflict theory is a fine template for analysing social relations, the lack of explanatory power strips it of its predictive power, which then remains limited to a remote notion of revolution, of overthrowing institutions or of 'smashing the patriarchy' in one go. It is often the case that patriarchy isn't smashed in one go. Instead, a series of individual acts—technological changes, cultural evolution, policy efforts and indeed protests too—smash the patriarchy little-by-little each time.

It is human ambition and action that lead to change and upward mobility. Change does not stop just because a theory fails to predict or explain it! Change does not stop because a theory says that it is impossible under the present conditions. Despite structural and theoretical constraints, change happens, often propelled by little more than ambition, technology, self-belief, the right values and a positive mindset.

It's true that women continue to face the worst kind of violence in this country. Every other day, we hear stories of rape, acid attacks, stalking and what not. The number of strategies that we employ as women to be safe in public spaces is mind-boggling—don't be out late, never let your phone run out of battery, only take the main roads and so on. However, this hasn't stopped women in India from marching ahead and claiming their space, even in the absence of any affirmative action from the state.

Similarly, it is true that Muslims are underrepresented in Parliament, but so are women and youth. But this hasn't stopped either women or youth from claiming their space in the knowledge economy. Muslims too, whenever equipped with the right skills, a positive mindset and educational credentials, have achieved stellar success, as the various stories in this book demonstrate. Muslim achievers haven't waited for political representation as a prerequisite to success. There are three key things to consider:

a) While greater representation is desirable, the mere fact of having political representation won't automatically change our socio–economic condition. It will still require a mindset shift, both in leadership as well as among people. The last seventy-five plus years have shown that our political leaders have only kept us backward by peddling orthodoxy in order to stay relevant.

b) Lack of political representation hasn't stopped any section of society from progressing, including Muslims, who are at the top in various fields.

c) It isn't Muslims alone who can represent us. An elected representative represents the entirety of his or her constituency. Non-Muslim leaders can represent us, just as Muslim achievers can be role models for all people, irrespective of faith.

If we have the drive, the right mindset, and the requisite skills, nobody can hold us back. The Sachar Committee Report in 2006 pointed out that the returns on higher education for Muslims are good and that the success rate in UPSC appointments is similar for Muslim candidates and other social groups.[6] Yes, we may face struggles, and some may even discriminate against us based on our name or appearance, but all that is temporary. Life is not fair to anyone, and we must not expect to be mollycoddled. Instead, we need to work on becoming indispensable through our knowledge, education and skills.

While it is no secret that the Modi government has not engaged in lip service at all, government initiatives such as the PM Vishwakarma scheme and PM SVANidhi scheme bring to fruition some of the Sachar Committee's recommendations related to tailored sectoral interventions and better credit flow in sectors where Muslims are predominantly engaged.[7] We need to make use of these schemes and also raise awareness within the community about the importance of higher education and futuristic skills. There is no cloud that can permanently hold back the sun from shining brightly, even if it may temporarily cast its shadow. We must work to make ourselves so strong that no one can cloud our brilliance beyond a certain point.

I am one of the most well-recognized voices in India in the field of activism and politics today, despite being a Kashmiri Muslim woman and despite having been the bitterest critic of the present-day government. The theories that I held on to for years convinced me that I shouldn't even be allowed to exist. But the fact is that I thrive because India is a nation built not on vendetta but on forgiveness, magnanimity, inclusivity, co-existence and tolerance—not only of religious views but also of political opinion.

I was forced to process these facts because they contradicted my worldview; therefore, I had to get rid of theories that had neither explanatory nor predictive power anymore. Even though my theory of change has evolved, the issues that I care about remain the same: the human rights of Kashmiris, the safety of women, the welfare of the poor, the development of Muslims and the overall progress of India.

My exit from left-leaning student activism was not a dramatic one. After my tenure as office-bearer of JNUSU ended in 2016, I kept searching for my theory of change within our constitutional framework, and I became convinced that we need to work at the regional level rather than in Delhi. So, as I've mentioned before, I made a brief foray into Kashmir politics, a move that came to a natural end on 5 August 2019 when the Government of India removed the special status of Jammu & Kashmir—a blow that made me go into a shell for four long years, including the pandemic year, during which I stopped commenting on issues and started observing them from a distance. Two developments led me to examine things afresh.

First was the unnecessary criticism of the government by critics over the Covid-19 pandemic lockdown. I asked myself as a citizen whether we really needed to oppose the government this time. Did the government have a choice but to impose a lock down? It was a classic damned if you do, damned if you don't situation for any government. I observed that the governments that enforced lockdown faced protests or criticism just as much as those that didn't. It was the same for mask mandates. Those who enforced mask mandates were called agents of a global conspiracy! I remember illustrious people engaging in such discourse when, in fact, it is in no government's security interest for people to mask up. Some things are beyond politics, but echo chambers and conspiracy theories do not allow us to see logic.

I found myself trying to use my platform to support the government's steps to control the spread of the virus. But I was shut down by people around me who asked me how I could support the government. No government on earth was prepared for it, and no government will want people to mask up in an age where facial recognition technology is promoted by governments. This is when I realized the effect of echo chambers, conspiracy theories and misinformation.

There were people who genuinely believed that Covid-19 was the handiwork of the 'Illuminati' or of global financial giants! However, stock markets around the world crashed, so it didn't sound logical. Also, it is not in capitalists' interests to halt production, so hearing otherwise smart people allege that Covid-19 was a capitalist trick was a bit surprising. Of all my achievements, I would say that the biggest one has been the ability to look outside the echo chamber and analyse things for myself. It is, after all, the power of rational inquiry that makes us human.

There was similar propaganda against Covid-19 vaccines, and I realized that anti-vaxxers have the luxury of being anti-vaxxers because, thanks to modern science, we have eradicated horrendous diseases such as smallpox and polio! Even constructivist scholar Bruno Latour, whose work forms the core of science and technology studies (STS) had to qualify his critique of science in view of the growing anti-science movement in the US.[8] Who knew that scientific advancement would lead us to a point where we would question science itself, as we are no longer faced with the prospect of dying from a deadly disease, affording us the luxury of thinking of a viral infection as a conspiracy?

Second, I noticed genuine positive change on the ground in Jammu & Kashmir in certain crucial areas: a) peace and security; b) the human rights situation; c) infrastructural development; d) governance reform; e) mindset shift and increased visibility of and space for women in the public sphere; f) transparency, accountability and fast-paced recruitments; and g) digitization of services. I, along with some others, had challenged the Government of India's move to remove Article 370 in the Supreme Court of India in 2019, believing that the move would lead to chaos, resentment and an uptick in insurgency. However, this radical move was followed up with strong developmental initiatives by the Centre and a strong security stance that deterred insurgent activities, stone-pelting, hartals and bandhs, poll boycotts, voter suppression through intimidation, etc.

What also helped turn the situation around was the able administration, large-heartedness and personal touch of Lt Gov. Manoj Sinha, whose political acumen and impartiality have rendered the real healing touch that Kashmir needed. We now have close to 300 business days and close to 200 working days in the academic calendar. Peace and security have led to enhanced investor confidence, ushering in high-quality infrastructural development in both the private and public sectors. Unprecedented railway linkages, the development of various new roads, flyovers and highways, high-profile events and MICE* tourism, including destination weddings, luxury car expos and car-racing events, are being witnessed.

From 2008 to 2016, Kashmir witnessed a never-ending cycle of stone-pelting, protests, killings of youth, etc. that gave credence to the language of human rights. However, speaking as a human rights activist, I would commend the Modi government's bold steps and decisive foreign policy for ending the cycle of violence and human rights violations in Kashmir. Today, even if some incident of human rights violation comes to the fore, it is dealt with swiftly.

While I was still a party to the constitutional challenge against the abrogation of Article 370, I would privately tell my friends, 'Yaar, I'll be lynched for saying this, but the Modi government has resolved Kashmir peacefully.' Eventually, I withdrew my name as a party to the constitutional challenge against the abrogation of Article 370 and I also went public with these views in 2023, as I believe in breaking silos and echo chambers when it is necessary. Not only did the changed facts on the ground lead me to re-examine my political beliefs, but also my academic stance.

While working on my PhD thesis, I started out with a critical orientation, bearing an anti-Aadhaar stance. However, what I observed is that India's Digital Public

---

* Meetings, incentives, conferences and exhibitions.

Infrastructure (DPI) has made welfare delivery more streamlined, following a kind of Kuznets curve, with initial hiccups resulting in denial of access to some, but eventually putting in place a systematic and targeted welfare delivery mechanism. And, as various authors in this book have pointed out, welfare has been delivered without discrimination. Innovative welfare schemes such as the Ayushman Bharat health insurance, the PM Janaushadhi (generic medicines) Yojana, etc., which are hugely successful in Kashmir, sit well with my left-leaning and pro-welfare beliefs.

Besides establishing peace in Kashmir and streamlining welfare delivery, I also observed positive developments in areas such as foreign policy where India's assertion of its strategic autonomy made sense to me, coming from a grounding in left politics that scoffs at alignment with any of the established power blocs. India's foreign minister, Dr S. Jaishankar has made generations of JNU alumni proud by bringing academic finesse to his political assignment. I believe that India is doing many things right, and we must contribute our bit too.

However, having the desire to contribute alone isn't enough. We need to be equipped with skills that are needed in the future and one of the most important skills that we need to develop is the ability to be prepared to be upskilled every few years if we are to compete! Hence, I have started doing my bit by initiating future-oriented skill-development projects for Kashmiri youth that make them ready to contribute to nation-building, while distinguishing themselves professionally. Contributing to the nation and the society does not have to be at odds with your own personal growth—the two are and should be complementary.

The move towards indigenization in various crucial sectors such as defence and semiconductors will open up opportunities for everyone—regardless of faith—in the coming decades. Investments in physical and DPI will empower everyone and enable innovation, growth and private initiative. We need to be prepared to take up these opportunities by upskilling ourselves, building our capacities, and leaning in to embrace this new vision for India. All of us must contribute our bit to building a Viksit Bharat by 2047, and this book is my humble attempt at working towards a mindset shift that can contribute to social harmony, inclusive development, and bridge-building.

Perspectives on Deprivation, Victimhood Narrative, Isolationism and Radicalization

—Amana Begam Ansari

- Amana Begam Ansari is a former research and policy analyst for the Delhi-based independent public policy think tank, the Citizens' Foundation for Policy Solutions, and a regular columnist for ThePrint India.
- She runs a YouTube channel called India This Week By Amana & Khalid.
- She has been raising her voice for Pasmanda Muslims as a member of the community.
- She recently completed her MBA in London.

Perception of Victimhood Among Indian Muslims

The perception of victimhood among Indian Muslims has been a persistent issue, shaping our socio–economic and political landscape[1]. While historical factors and social dynamics contribute to this perception, a comprehensive analysis reveals that the exclusion of Indian Muslims is not primarily rooted in systematic discrimination but is largely a consequence of the perception of victimhood itself. The Sachar Committee Report (2006) documented in detail this perception of victimhood and the resulting reluctance to participate and compete in the national mainstream[2]. An important consequence of this perception is that Indian Muslims perceive a lack of returns from education, therefore assigning low importance to secular education[3]. The Report itself concludes that this perception is wrong, noting that the returns are higher for higher levels of education (as it should be)[4].

The perception of victimhood erodes the faith of the community in institutions, processes and even in the democratic process, as a result of which people disengage from mainstream institutions, government schemes, competitive exams and nation-building. This sense of alienation can create fertile ground for radicalization, as disenfranchised individuals may seek alternative ideologies or groups that offer a sense of belonging or empowerment. Without avenues for constructive participation or outlets for grievances, some individuals may resort to rebellious or extremist behaviour as a means of expressing their frustrations or seeking redress for perceived injustices. The tendency to assign low value to education is a classic example of a mindset arising out of poverty, which makes long-term planning and investment difficult.

The 'Culture of Poverty' thesis put forth by Oscar Lewis in 1966 suggests that poverty is not merely a result of economic deprivation but is also a product of a distinct set of cultural values, attitudes, and behaviours that perpetuate poverty across generations.[5] In the 'Culture of Poverty' thesis, Oscar Lewis argued that individuals experiencing poverty develop a set of learned behaviours and attitudes often shaped by their socio–economic circumstances. These may include a sense of hopelessness, a lack of long-term planning and limited access to educational and economic opportunities.

Similarly, the Rich Dad, Poor Dad thesis, put forth by Robert Kiyosaki, draws attention to the contrast between a poverty-driven mindset, characterized by financial dependence and risk aversion on the one hand, and a wealth-building mindset, marked by financial literacy, entrepreneurial spirit, and strategic investment on the other[6]. Both perspectives highlight the profound influence that one's mindset and beliefs can have on economic outcomes, underscoring the importance of addressing not only the material aspects of poverty but also the **psychological and cultural dimensions to break the cycle of generational poverty.**

In the Indian context, this is commonly observed in the tendency among the educationally and economically backward classes—across faiths—to have a number of children without having the resources to educate them, in the hope that the children will soon contribute financially to the family through their labour. However, in the absence of education and skills, work is usually less rewarding and hazardous, trapping the family in a spiral of low wages, debt, disease, vulnerability to injury and a resulting erosion of savings.

In case of poor Muslims, there is a preference for deeni education over dunyawi learning. This is one of the behaviours that I would group under 'isolationism' and I will attempt to explain why and how an isolationist worldview results in exclusion. Parents prefer to send children to study in institutions where deeni *taleem* (religious instruction) can be imparted, but these institutions cannot be an alternative to formal schooling. As per the 2011 census, 40 per cent of Muslims haven't attended formal schooling.[7] Children in madrasas aren't fully exposed to the competition that they will face in coming years. This causes Muslim children to lag behind in today's competitive age.

Nowadays, formal schooling begins at a very early age with the explosion of preschools. As early as two and a half years of age, kids start to attend playschools and parents insist that skills such as foreign languages, playing a musical instrument, coding, etc. be imparted very early. By contrast, kids attending madrasas do not even get the exposure of basic formal schooling, let alone finer skills and, as a result, tend to lag significantly behind their peers in terms of life chances.

The resulting wide skill gap between Muslim students and their peers leads to lifelong **exclusion**. Such intergenerational disparities in class and status lead to stratification—a fact that is then weaponized by those who want to rally Muslims for votes, not allowing the community to look deeper into the causes of it.

In cases where Muslim youth do manage to attain higher education, they find the severe underrepresentation of their community in higher educational institutions disturbing and they may search for answers in theory. The only comparable framework appears to be critical race theory (CRT), which systematically examines the stratified nature of American society on the basis of race. There is, then, a tendency to extrapolate this framework to Indian society based on parallels such as residential segregation, even though there is no racial divide between Muslims and non-Muslims in India. Thus, exclusion and segregation create an **objective, empirical basis for a perception of victimhood** among Muslims, leading to attraction to **radical ideologies** and/or **conflict theories** (such as Marxism).

Due to the apparent conflict between Marxism and faith, some university students may find themselves attracted to liberation theology, which blends Marxism and faith and insists that justice is a prerequisite to peace (in other words, violence is a legitimate means in the face of perceived injustice). In the age of social media, youth may become part of information silos that selectively feed them information about crimes against Muslims, furthering the hold of radical ideologies and isolation. Furthermore, the collaboration between religious and so-called 'modern' leadership with Muslim names, alongside liberal-secular-left forces, perpetuates an industry of victimhood. This alliance utilizes identity-based victimhood narratives for political gain, exploiting them in electoral strategies and for continued political relevance.

This is not to suggest that instances of actual discrimination or real violence against Muslims are absent in India. However, taking real injustices as a causal factor for radicalization is a logical fallacy because radicalization exists in Pakistan too, which is a nation exclusively for Muslims. Yet, there is a trend of Muslim youth in higher educational institutions in Pakistan being drawn to radicalization[8]. Here too, there is a narrative of 'injustice' despite the absence of any other faith group. Hence, radicalization has more to do with storytelling.

What is common to radical organizations everywhere is a narrative of injustice which is used to indoctrinate and brainwash young recruits. Hence, the use of the term victimhood 'perception' as opposed to actual 'injustice'. It is a 'perception' of victimhood, a narrative of injustice, that contains the seed of extremism, not necessarily the actual instances of injustice itself. We haven't seen any family of a victim of mob lynching pick up the gun. In fact, we have often heard them talk about reconciliation and coexistence. Instead, a second-hand narrative of 'injustice' arising out of socio-economic exclusion of the community which is, in turn, driven by isolationist tendencies in large part, is the real driver of radicalization.

Addressing the victimhood perception, therefore, becomes crucial in preventing the radicalization of Muslim youth, which raises concerns for internal security as well as national security. Radicalization needn't always be associated with extremism or violence, which require a further leap and, often, grooming by an extremist or violent organization. However, even self-radicalization on its own is enough to perpetuate further isolation, which leads to exclusion from mainstream society even if one possesses the right skills and education. One such example is that of Sharjeel Imam, who was not part of any student group at the university and was a mere free-floating individual. But self-radicalization led him to allegedly make comments inimical to national security and communal harmony and get jailed, even though he is not involved with any radical organization. For an ordinary Muslim youth, watching highly educated Muslim youth like him get jailed furthers a sense of victimhood, leading to conclusions about the futility and pointlessness of higher education, leading to the self-fulfilling prophecy that, 'even if Muslims get educated, they will still end up in jail', completing the circle by furthering reluctance towards higher education.

The Need for Reform Among Muslims

Let's admit it, the transformation of the last ten years has not been an easy one for us as minorities. Many of our parochial beliefs have been challenged, including our defence of the indefensible Article 35-A in Jammu & Kashmir and abhorrent practices such as triple talaq. We have been forced to confront these social evils that have rendered women subordinate. Reform must be initiated from within the community; otherwise, the state will be forced to intervene. At times, when censure from within the community is too strong, it may be in our interest to accept reform initiated by the state. They are, after all, doing the hard job for us in such cases.

The onus was on us as a community to remove discriminatory practices against women, yet we failed to rise to the occasion time and again, be it in the Shah Bano case*, the triple talaq issue or retrograde practices

---

* The Shah Bano case (1985) was a landmark judgment in India where the Supreme Court granted maintenance to a divorced Muslim

legitimized by 'personal' law such as polygamy or the unilateral rights of men to divorce their wives, and so on. The issue often is that the leaders of our community are the religious preachers, the orthodox maulanas, who may not be radicalized but are quite simply unaware, uneducated and illiberal by virtue of their lack of exposure. Yet, these are the people who end up preaching to us and representing us, as nobody else is allowed to have a voice. Anyone from within the community who dares to speak up against any of the prevalent practices, such as loudspeakers in mosques, etc., will be deemed an apostate and hence a target. Fatwas will be issued on his or her religiosity, leading to total censure and even a threat to life. Hence, we need to define newer role models who can represent the aspirational Indian Muslim—a Muslim 'civil society', as Shehla Rashid aptly puts it.

History is witness to the fact that those who fail to reform fail to flourish. Similarly, the Holy Qur'an 13:11 underscores that Allah will not alter the circumstances of people until they change themselves—'Verily, Allah does not change the condition of a people until they change what is within themselves.'[9] We can complain

---

woman under Section 125 of the Criminal Procedure Code. This verdict challenged the provisions of Muslim personal law regarding women's rights and ignited a national debate on the Uniform Civil Code. While the judgment was initially hailed as a progressive step, subsequent political pressure led to the passage of the Muslim Women (Protection of Rights on Divorce) Act, 1986 which overturned the Supreme Court's decision, limiting maintenance to a limited period.

about Islamophobia all we want, but we must admit that the lack of internal reform, the inability to rein in religious extremism and the tendencies of illiberalism have earned Muslims a bad name in today's world, which is the world of open, democratic societies. The aspirational Indian Muslim wants equality, not special treatment by politicians who offer lip service to our causes, attracting accusations of 'appeasement'. We need to define our own role models who are forward-looking, progressive and reform oriented.

The European Enlightenment paved the way for progress, science and advances in modern medicine and industry—basically, everything that we use today to conduct our modern lives. It is true that the Golden Age of Islam preceded the European Enlightenment by several centuries, but it does not suffice to say that we were the first to invent algebra or alchemy in our defence. It is important to ask why we went from being a scientifically oriented people to one preoccupied with dogmas and doctrinal totalitarianism rather than the doctrinal pluralism that marked the Golden Age of Islam[10]. It is also important to ask how this hindered our growth. The modern world is democratic and open, so even theocracies such as Saudi Arabia are endorsing reform. In order to progress, we will have to keep up with the times. The core tenets of Islam are faith (shahadat), prayer (salat), charity (zakat), fasting (roza) and pilgrimage to Mecca and Medina if possible (hajj). Loudspeakers, triple talaq, polygamy, etc. are not core symbols of faith and have been rejected by many Muslim-majority nations.

Most practising Muslims privately acknowledge that loudspeakers in mosque pulpits are a nuisance, even a *biddat* (innovation) not prevalent in the Prophet (PBUH)'s time. In 2021, Saudi Arabia directed all mosques to limit the volume of loudspeakers to one-third of their maximum volume.[11] In an age where we use mobile phones and digital alarms and reminders for everything—even for drinking water—why do we need loudspeakers to remind us of prayers? Why can't we have an app for the same? But even a much-needed and agreed-upon reform such as this becomes a question of 'Who will bell the cat?' Similarly, most practicing Muslims privately state that praying on the roadside is frowned upon in the Hadith and Fiqh*. However, we hold on lazily to these practices, whereas nowhere in any Islamic country is it allowed to pray on the roads. In 2017, Dubai for instance introduced a fine for praying on roads, but here we are afraid of expressing such views[12].

Trembling with fear and suffocated by censorship, the community is held hostage by the power of a select few who arrogantly issue fatwas, branding those who dare to question innovative practices as apostates, heretics or blasphemers. The authoritarian inclinations within our faith are driving people away

---

* Fiqh means Islamic jurisprudence.

from religion, evident in the burgeoning 'ex-Muslim' movement, particularly on social media. The idea that contemporary Islamic practices are a line etched in stone, impossible to reform, drives people away from Islam because it becomes a statement of the impossibility of reform within the ambit of faith. However, the current government's efforts to catalyse reform within the Muslim community offer a glimmer of hope, potentially shielding us from our own self-destructive tendencies.

There is growing consensus among Muslim intellectuals that we must not become tools in the hands of political parties and must engage with governments in a non-adversarial way. We may criticize certain policies rightfully as citizens, but our perennial opposition to mainstream narratives positions us as self-declared enemies of government, preventing us from having a constructive voice. It makes us emotional and gullible, and therefore more vulnerable to being subjected to misinformation or partial information by media outlets that play to our confirmation bias and gullibility. When we view the whole situation through a detached lens, we are able to judge rationally and criticize logically. While the critics of the government in our community are vocal, those who insist on focusing on professional excellence while accepting the democratic mandate prefer a stoic silence for fear of being branded 'sarkari Musalman' (literal: establishment Muslim). There is a need to state that we, as a community, cannot progress by perennially being in anti-establishment mode either. This is not a call to be apolitical, but to be political in the right ways.

If the opposition—any opposition party—can provide an alternative to an incumbent government's policies, forming something like a shadow cabinet and informing the electorate about what they will do differently on various counts, we may support them. After all, Muslim citizens care about all kinds of issues—from environment, foreign policy, women's safety and healthcare to industrial policy, as this book shows.

In the last ten years, India has witnessed an undeniable, unmistakable and remarkable transformation in the spheres of digital governance, financial inclusion, foreign policy and strategic affairs, welfare provision, peace and security, transport and logistics, sports and athletics, telecom, road connectivity and many other fields. There is no dearth of statistical data and qualitative evidence to back it up. Muslims have benefited from these initiatives just as every other citizen has. India's investment in and expansion of public infrastructure, both physical and digital, in the last decade is something that all classes of citizens will benefit from, Muslims included, for generations to come.

Cynics are likely to say that one swallow does not a summer make. I would say that one flamingo does not a winter make either. The story is somewhere in between. We will need to rid ourselves of extreme narratives and step outside echo chambers to acknowledge the new heights to which India is rising. Perennial and permanent cynicism leads to polarization.

Communal harmony is a two-way street. We must build bridges with other communities at the local level, acting together as citizens. Some organizations, such as the Chishty Foundation (of Ajmer Sharif) and the Indian Minorities Foundation, are filling the vacuum by organizing inter-faith harmony programmes. This effort must be replicated throughout the Muslim community. We cannot insist on Hindus alone being liberal and following constitutionalism while we continue being communal and following a Sharia-inspired reasoning. We cannot insist that only Hindus have secular, tolerant and constitutionalist thinking while we continue to derive our reasoning, worldview and political choices from Sharia. It is convenient to say that the onus to accommodate and integrate is on the majority, but logically, the incentive to do so is more for a minority community than for the majority.

We often like to boast that 'Islam is the fastest-growing religion in the United States' but this is possible because liberal, tolerant and open societies often serve as better avenues for Islam to flourish due to the moderating influence of democratic and this-worldly cultures such as Hinduism and liberal Protestantism. Extremist tendencies are a negative advertisement for faith, driving people away from Islam. For instance, Iran's recent anti-Hijab movement grew as a result of totalitarian Islam. In the absence of moderating influences, people are in fact repelled by faith.

Every now and then, we see atheists in Muslim nations being jailed or attacked for alleged blasphemy or simply for following a different sect.[13] The endless list of conflicts in the Middle East shows us that Muslims are safer in non-Muslim nations than in Muslim nations. Hence, it might be fair to say that both Islam and Muslims are more likely to flourish in non-Muslim nations, as the latter are secular by virtue of having undergone reform. Therefore, we should not see reforms as attacks on our faith. The Muslim population in India has increased from 10 per cent at the time of independence to over 14 per cent now.[14] Hence, we must have faith in the greatness of this country and work to preserve this greatness. We shouldn't let one stray incident define our entire view of Hinduism or of India. Just like every Muslim is not a terrorist, every Hindu is not a zealot.

A Way Forward: Fostering Inclusive Development

A government that insists on fighting Islamic extremism needs to take members of Muslim civil society along as allies, because every person who has risen to prominence in their respective field has had to put up a fight against familial or social orthodoxy.

Unwarranted attacks on Muslim public figures, asking them to go to Pakistan and calling them 'jihadis' defeats the project of promoting civilizational unity among various communities in India. Such actions not only undermine our potential as agents of reform but also reflect the very extremism we vehemently oppose, jeopardizing our credibility and moral standing.

Muslims must seek systematic support from the government, and the government must ensure impartial and inclusive development, providing support to the most marginalized and deserving communities, such as Pasmanda Muslims and Muslim women. We must hold the state and its institutions accountable, seek basic support, try to benefit from schemes and government programmes and use such support to better our lives and make better, rational choices.

Empowering Muslim Youth

The key to breaking the cycle lies in empowering Muslim youth through inclusive development initiatives. The government, particularly the present government, can play a pivotal role in fostering participation and dismantling the victimhood narrative, as successive BJP governments have followed a model of **principled engagement** with the Muslim community, which marks a departure from the earlier model of appeasement and provides a shield to conservative practices. Empowering Muslim communities to advocate for their rights and interests is essential for challenging systemic inequalities. Encouraging civic engagement, grassroots organizing and political participation can amplify Muslim voices and promote representation in decision-making processes.

Skill Development and Capacity Building

Investing in skill development and capacity-building programmes is essential. Initiatives tailored towards the futuristic skills required in the IT industry can bridge the existing employment gap. The recommendation here is to **leverage existing initiatives and use them for greater outreach to the community**. The various skills listed under the PM Vishwakarma Yojana are aligned with various traditional occupations pursued by Pasmanda Muslims and will be helpful in their mainstreaming.

Empowering Muslim Women

Women's empowerment is not just a matter of equality; it is a fundamental prerequisite for the well-being and prosperity of any community. As Desmond Tutu once said, 'There is no tool for development more effective than the empowerment of women.' When women are empowered, they become agents of change, driving progress in education, health, economic development and social cohesion. By investing in women's education, healthcare and economic opportunities, communities can unlock their full potential and achieve sustainable development. Empowered women are not only able to improve their own lives but also uplift their families, communities and societies as a whole.

The time has indeed arrived for Indian Muslims to actively engage in reform efforts within society, particularly concerning the empowerment of women. The BJP's initiatives, such as the ban on triple talaq and various empowerment schemes, signal a step in the right direction towards fostering gender equality within the Muslim community. The election of Kausar Jahan, a BJP member, as the chair of the Delhi State Haj Committee sends a positive message, highlighting the potential for Muslim women to assume leadership roles and contribute meaningfully to decision-making processes. By embracing such opportunities and advocating for women's rights, Indian Muslims can play a pivotal role in shaping a more inclusive and equitable society for all.

Empowering India's Pasmanda Muslims for Inclusion and Equality

The plight of the Pasmanda Muslim communities in India remains one of political, social, and economic marginalization, affecting approximately 90 per cent of the Muslim population. Historically, during medieval times, indigenous peoples, including Adivasis, Scheduled Castes and Backward Castes, converted to Islam from Buddhism and Hinduism, comprising 85 per cent of the total Muslim demographic[15]. Contrary to common misconceptions, only a small fraction, around 3–4 per cent, of Muslims are of foreign origin, with approximately 10 per cent being converts from upper castes. This reality underscores the fact that the vast majority of Muslims in India are of Indian origin, with the marginalized remnants referred to as Pasmandas or the ignored ones. Given this context, it is imperative to prioritize efforts aimed at working with and uplifting these communities to address their longstanding socio-economic challenges and ensure their inclusion and empowerment in contemporary society.

Conclusion: Breaking the cycle of Muslim victimhood and marginalization is a complex and multifaceted challenge that requires sustained commitment and collaboration from all sectors of society and a concerted effort from multiple stakeholders, including governments, civil society organizations, religious leaders and the broader community.

Acknowledgements

A few years ago, when I spoke at Columbia University's School of International and Public Affairs (SIPA), I had the privilege of visiting Dr B.R. Ambedkar's bronze bust at SIPA's Lehman Social Sciences Library. Despite being a member of a marginalized community from a colonized nation, Dr Ambedkar earned a double doctorate in Economics from both Columbia and London School of Economics (LSE), shattering numerous stereotypes in the process. Achieving academic distinction as a scholar of colour in America well before the civil rights movement, before even white women could vote, was no small feat. Not to mention his role as the shaper of India's Constitution. No wonder he is held up as a role model and a father figure by Dalit scholars worldwide, for whom he serves as an aspirational standard.

It filled me with pride to see an Indian being celebrated so far away from home, while also prompting me to think about such a figure from among Indian Muslims who is similarly celebrated and universally accepted. Though an easy read, my book explores this crucial question, offering various possible role models whom we can look up to. I became interested in this question because when we see someone like us achieve something like that, we dare to dream. It shapes our aspirational matrix, broadening the horizons of what we believe we can achieve, setting us up for success. In sociology, there is considerable interest in the power of role models—whether distant or proximate, real or fictional—in shaping our goals.

Growing up, my own role model was Helen Keller, the first American person with deafblindness to earn a Bachelor of Arts degree. Her story has been a source of strength for me throughout my life. My own mother has also been a role model for me. A true-blue Leo, she is strong as a rock and a fraction of it may have rubbed off on me too. As a student of Sociology at JNU prestigious Centre for the Study of Social Systems (CSSS), I was introduced to role model theory which studies the impact of inspirational community figures in driving upward mobility, especially among marginalized or minority communities. All these influences combined inform this book.

This book is also an outcome of the desire to simply shine a light on the contributions of Indian Muslims, something that is starkly missing from both public discourse as well as popular culture. We often see negative depictions of Muslims in movies, but we haven't seen any movies depicting a Muslim philanthropist (such as Azim Premji) or a freedom fighter (such as Badruddin Tyabji or Ashfaqullah Khan). Not only does this shape perceptions about Muslims amongst the larger populace, but it also signals to the Muslim community to coalesce around such depictions, making us identify subconsciously with the said representations. This book attempts to change that, bringing to light some remarkable stories of Indian Muslim achievers, some would say over-achievers!

Ever since I embarked upon this project, I have received nothing but encouragement, for which I'm grateful. Whoever heard the idea loved it instantly, wondering why no such book exists. In that sense, this book—much like its contributors—is in a league of its own! I'm thankful to all the contributors who spared their valuable time for this project despite their busy schedules. I'm grateful to God for choosing me as the protagonist of this incredibly important narrative and for giving me the opportunity to speak to so many distinguished and inspiring people.

I am especially grateful to A.R. Rahman sahab who has, for the first time, lent his voice to a book project, recognizing the dire need for a positive narrative about Muslims. Despite being in the middle of various projects, he took out time and bore with my constant badgering. This book provides a rare insight into his genius mind and humble persona.

I am also deeply grateful to Salim Khan sahab, who was kind enough to host me and my team at his residence, showing us artefacts from his life and playing beautiful Raj Kapoor songs for us, which was an unforgettable experience. He gave us his blessings and cheered us up at a time when this project had started to look impossible. His encouragement was uplifting, to say the least.

I'm also grateful to Sania Mirza and her team for the professional and timely manner in which she contributed to this project. I was blown away by the humility of Nigar Shaji ma'am of the ISRO, an unassuming genius. I'm honoured to have Huma Qureshi participate in this project, despite her busy shooting schedule for Season 3 of *Maharani*.

I must thank my mother and sister for always being there for me, especially through the last four years as I struggled with numerous stress-induced health issues. I am grateful for their unconditional love and support, which propelled me to outstanding success and a terrific comeback following years of isolation. My sister also helped me brutally edit my own essay, giving crucial input and feedback.

I'm grateful to Shams Aalam, whose story inspired me to ask myself, 'What's your excuse?' every time I experienced burnout while working on the book. It has been truly inspiring to work on his essay. I'm thankful to Dr Jamal Khan for constantly motivating me through his kind words whenever it seemed that things weren't working out.

I would like to thank Nabiha Zama, Jatan Mehta and Dr Adil Malik for providing research assistance. I'm grateful to Rama Singh Durgvanshi and Ankur Garg for facilitating a couple of timely connections. While some of my friends may not like to be named here, they have been my advisers and sounding boards throughout this process, offering valuable feedback, strategic advice and generally listening to me. You know who you are.

Finally, I'd like to thank Penguin Random House India for sticking with me through everything. I'm grateful to the editorial team at PRH for their meticulous work on the manuscript.

This book project was supported by a writing grant from the Indian Minorities Foundation.

Appendix

Ever since I appeared on a podcast with Smita Prakash on ANI in November 2023, where I praised the Modi government's decisive steps in Jammu and Kashmir, I am often asked by people I meet what the 'true situation' in Jammu and Kashmir is. Since this book is about Indian Muslim achievers, I did not want to digress too much from the topic. So, for reasons of argument flow, I have added this appendix to substantiate the assertions using both qualitative as well as quantitative information.

Public memory in Kashmir is divided into pre-abrogation and post-abrogation phases. It is well-known that, in the pre-abrogation phase, whenever ordinary Kashmiris were asked who was the 'best Prime Minister', they'd fondly recall Late Vajpayee ji. The reason is simple. He was seen by Kashmiris as the only Prime Minister who sincerely tried to resolve the Kashmir issue. Mr. Vajpayee spoke of all possible solutions within the ambit of 'Kashmiriyat, Jamhooriyat, and Insaniyat'. While the Modi government has gone truly out-of-the-box in resolving the Kashmir issue by abrogating Article 370, what needs to be stressed is that the solution also fits the parameters of Kashmiriyat, Jamhooriyat and Insaniyat.

Article 370 and 35A were socially regressive. Post-abrogation, I would go to Boulevard Road by the Dal Lake for a morning run as all gymnasia were closed due to COVID. We were stunned to find girls in workout gear walking, cycling and running. This was a landmark shift for us. Growing up in Kashmir meant facing immense moral policing for simple things that we take for granted in Delhi and other cities, like wearing jeans. Recalling this now seems like a déjà vu from a past life, but that is exactly what the abrogation has done—made orthodoxy and moral policing a thing of the past, along with Article 35-A, which denied women who married outside the state the right to dispose of their property as they wished.

Let's now examine the impact of abrogation in light of the Vajpayee parameters.

Insaniyat (Humanity): Nobody could have imagined that the solution to the Kashmir issue or even the removal of Article 35-A would be a bloodless event. However, the forward march of history does not stop just because theory failed to explain or predict it. Not only was the abrogation bloodless, but its aftermath has also seen a steady decline in violence and bloodshed. Terrorist attacks in the Valley reduced from 228 in 2018 to 41 in 2023. The number of civilians killed in terrorism-related incidents decreased from 55 in 2018 to 13 in 2023. The number of security personnel killed in action fell from 91 in 2018 to 20 in 2023. There's an unmistakable perception of security and peace which has enabled more economic activity, physical movement of people till late hours even in winter, increased investments including by local businessmen, and a palpable reduction in fear psychosis. This has been made possible by the government's zero tolerance approach to terrorism, cracking down on the entire 'ecosystem' of terror and not just its symptoms.

Jamhooriyat (Democracy): The government is slowly creating a space where political opinions can be expressed without fear of reprisal, censorship or gun violence. Democracy is, foremost, a marketplace of political opinions. But the freedom to hold political opinion was held hostage to soft separatism, which was the key formula to surviving in politics without fear of being shot. The government is creating space for genuine democracy to flourish and not just a stage-managed show of elite politicians who are protected by a mix of state machinery and soft separatism. The government, by ensuring elections to all levels of Panchayati Raj Institutions (PRIs), has created over 27,000 stakeholders in the democratic process. Over

9000 of these elected representatives are women, thereby ushering in a critical mass of grassroots women leaders who, in the future, will form the cohort of empowered women seeking representation in legislatures once the 106th Constitutional Amendment Act comes into force. The Lok Sabha election held in 2024 was a free, fair and transparent process—which is significant given the fact that insurgency in Kashmir was a direct result of widespread election rigging in 1987. A record number of voters participated, and a candidate lodged in Tihar Jail won by record margins. Now, assembly elections are being held, and the restoration of all three tiers of government will be a reality soon.

Kashmiriyat: Nearly two crore tourists visited Kashmir in 2023, and Srinagar city proudly hosted the G-20 meeting, signaling confidence and cooperation between the security establishment and the masses. No incidents of stone-pelting have been reported in 2023 and 2024. For the first time in thirty years, the full academic calendar was followed in both years. There have been no hartals, curfews or strikes. Schools and colleges have been able to function without disruption. For the first time in decades, Muharram processions by Shia mourners were allowed under the Lt Gov. Manoj Sinha administration, ensuring freedom of religion for *all* Muslims.

Besides this, government processes have been streamlined and institutions have become more accessible. Recruitments are happening at a record pace and in a transparent manner. As many as 31,380 selections (Gazetted and Non-Gazetted) have been finalized by the recruiting agencies since 2019. The Lt Gov.'s administration has instituted enquiries against erring cops, addressed concerns of candidates around the integrity of JKSSB exams by blacklisting the erring companies and integrated 914 online services with the Rapid Assessment System (RAS) whereby citizens who have accessed a service can submit feedback regarding their experience, along with a system of auto-escalation. Institutions are functioning for everyone regardless of political patronage.

With an increasing number of services being successfully digitized, citizens are coming to depend less and less on personal influence, proving conventional wisdom about e-governance right. The Back to Village programme has been a spectacular success as the government delivered G2C services at people's doorstep, with senior officials visiting villages rather than citizens visiting government offices. Welfare schemes such as Ayushman Bharat, Pradhan Mantri Awas Yojana, Pradhan Mantri Ujjwala Yojana, etc. have touched the lives of numerous Labharthis.

Public infrastructure has received a visible facelift with state-of-the-art transport, heritage conservation, decongestion and renovation work being done at a fast pace. The breathtaking Chenab Rail bridge in the Reasi district is the highest railway bridge in the world, built at a height of 1178 ft. above the river, 35 m taller than the Eiffel tower. Investment figures have seen a ten-fold spike from Rs 296.64 crore in FY'20 to Rs 2079.76 crore in FY'24 up to 31 October 2023. A visible uptick in private enterprise is attributable to peace and investor confidence.

Governance issues such as power cuts, waste management, unemployment, stray dog issue, etc. need redressal. But the integration of Jammu & Kashmir with mainland India has ended the psychological duality of the residents of the Valley which, while a measure for greater federalism within the Indian Republic, served to boost separatism by providing for a separate Constitution, a separate penal code, and a separate flag. People can now be seen participating enthusiastically in festivities such as the Independence Day and the Republic Day. The academic session has been synced with the March session followed in the rest of India, as opposed to the earlier system which caused students from Jammu and Kashmir to lose a year compared to their counterparts in the rest of the country.

Security challenges remain, especially the targeted killings of police personnel and the shifting of terror incidents to the Pir Panjal area. One of the aims of terrorist actions (globally speaking) is to provoke the country which is at the receiving end of violence into a reaction which inevitably results in missteps, collateral damage and human rights violations. These real injustices are then exploited by advocacy lobbies which are in cahoots with the original aggressor group or country to portray the party at the receiving end of terrorism as the villain. Without this understanding of international relations, it is difficult to make sense of seemingly 'mindless' acts of terrorism which are not so mindless after all.

While insurgency in the Muslim-majority Kashmir division has dwindled, incidents of infiltration have picked up pace in the Hindu-majority Jammu division. Constant provocations, attacks on pilgrims, ambushed security personnel every now and then are likely to send security forces on a wild goose chase in order to look for infiltrators in the thick forests of the Pir Panjal range. This will inevitably involve questioning and interrogation of locals who are suspected collaborators. During this process, it is not rare to expect an emotional response from soldiers whose comrades have been ambushed. If any human rights violations take place during this, as they sometimes do, these are exploited by the international human rights lobbies which won't bother to call out the original sponsor of terrorism.

Thus, the terrorist acts in Jammu require a calibrated response which takes on board locals and empowers them in the fight against terrorism, so that the resentment that my generation grew up with is not handed down to future generations. It is, in fact, a result of improvements in Kashmir that the site of mischief has moved to Jammu which is closer to the border and much easier to infiltrate. If Kashmir had been the preferred site so far for infiltration, owing to local support, Jammu is now the more practical route for infiltrators, owing to proximity. All this is likely to create friction between civilians and security forces in the Jammu region, an issue-based resentment that can get channeled into a larger anti-India sentiment among the locals.

Keeping in view the larger geopolitics of Pak-sponsored terrorism, India must carve out a bigger role for Muslims especially when it comes to articulating our national security position and strategic objectives, both domestically and globally—a kind of 'Muslim para-diplomacy' if you will—leveraging our diversity as a diplomatic strength. This book is a humble attempt to showcase the diversity and openness of India. Between the dozen odd people featured in this book, they share six civilian honours of the highest level that are awarded by the government of India. Muslims can aspire to reach the highest positions in all fields including the military. After all, how many non-Islamic countries can boast of having Muslim army generals? We have had not one but many Muslims as army generals, three Muslim presidents, numerous Bollywood stars, and so on. This diversity needs to be showcased and celebrated.

Notes

Introduction

1 R.K. Merton, *Social Theory and Social Structure* (Free Press, 1949).

2 A. Bandura, *Social Learning Theory* (Prentice-Hall, 1977).

3 While the motivational theory of role modeling is generally applicable to young people, it has been studied more often among minoritized communities, such as people of African descent in the US. (Morgenroth, Ryan, and Peters, 2015).

4 T. Morgenroth, M.K. Ryan and K. Peters, 'The Motivational Theory of Role Modeling: How Role Models Influence Role Aspirants' Goals', *Review of General Psychology* 19(4) (2015): 465–483. https://doi.org/10.1037/gpr0000059

5 *Sachar Committee Report: Social, economic and educational status of the Muslim Community of India; A report, Prime Minister's High Level Committee*, Cabinet Secretariat, Government of India, 2006, https://www.minorityaffairs. gov.in/WriteReadData/RTF1984/7830578798.pdf

6 Sachar Committee Report (2006), pp. 91–92.

7   'C-09: Educational level by religious community and sex for population age 7 and above, 2011', Government of India Census Digital Library, 10 July 2024 https://censusindia.gov.in/nada/index.php/catalog/2493

8   'All India Survey on Higher Education (AISHE), 2021-22', Ministry of Education, Government of India, p. 40. https://cdnbbsr.s3waas.gov.in/s392049debbe566ca5782a3045cf300a3c/uploads/2024/02/20240719952688509.pdf or here: https://aishe.gov.in/

9   Sachar Committee Report (2006), pp. 221-235.

10 Sachar Committee Report (2006), p. 23.

11 Raza Rumi, 'Sayyid Ahmad Khan's Search for a Modern Muslim', Hudson Institute, 1 October 2022, https://www.hudson.org/terrorism/sayyid-ahmad-khans-search-modern-muslim

12 Najid Hussain, 'Kalam and Islam', *Outlook*, 18 July, 2002, Archived at https://web.archive.org/web/20151031225107/https://www.outlookindia.com/article/kalam-and-islam/216493

13 The said article stirred a huge debate back in 2002, but has since been removed from the Internet. References to it can be found in Najid Hussain's Outlook article referenced above and its text is available on various online forums. It is also referenced in Varsha Bhosle's *Rediff* article titled 'Carefully constructed facades'. Dr Kalam once responded to this debate in an interview with M. J. Akbar in 2012 which is accessible online https://www.indiatoday.in/magazine/interview/story/20120709-abdul-kalam-presidential-elections-2012-new-book-turning-points-758940-2012-06-29

14 Sidharth MP, 'Overcoming grief after parents' demise, Dr. Kalam led launch of India's first rocket SLV-3', *WION*, 15 Oct, 2023, https://www.wionews.com/science/

overcoming-parents-demise-dr-kalam-led-launch-of-indias-first-rocket-slv-3-647052

15 The article titled 'The Burden of an unheroic hero' by Omair Ahmed published on 17 February 2020 was retracted by Outlook on account of a derogatory reference made in it, for which the publication apologised.

16 M Ilyas Khan, '*Why has this Nobel winner been ignored for 30 years?*', *BBC*, 8 December, 2016 https://www.bbc.com/news/world-asia-38238131

17 Sachar Committee Report (2006), pp. 15-16

18 Sachar Committee Report (2006), p. 219.

19 Sachar Committee Report (2006), p. 220.

20 Source: https://azimpremjiuniversity.edu.in/azim-premji-foundation

Embody the Change You Want to See

1 Richard Corliss, 'All-TIME 100 Movies: 10 Best Soundtracks—Roja', *TIME*, 19 Jan, 2010, https://entertainment.time.com/2005/02/12/all-time-100-movies/slide/roja/

2 'Grammys nominations full winners nominees list', *Recording Academy*, https: //www.grammy.com/news/2024-grammysnominations-full-winners-nominees-list

The Sky Is No Longer the Limit for India

1 "Amrit Peedhi" to take India to new heights: PM Modi to 'GenZ', *Hindustan Times*, 24 January 2024, https://www.hindustantimes.com/india-news/amrit-peedhi-to-take-india-to-new-heights-pm-modi-to-genz-101706094982599.html

On Grand Slams, Girl Power and Building a Better India

1   'Sachin Tendulkar, 'An inspiration on the court'', *TIME*, 21 April, 2016, https://time.com/collection-post/4298231/sania-mirza-2016-time-100/

So, What's Your Excuse?

1   https://balswavlambantrust.org/active-x-wheelchair/
2   Dimension of Disability in India, in '*Disability in India- A Statistical Profile-2011*', Ministry of Statistics and Programme Implementation, Government of India, pp. D1. https://www.mospi.gov.in/publication/disability-india-statistical-profile-2011-1
3   https://www.who.int/en/news-room/fact-sheets/detail/disability-and-health
4   https://www.wethe15.org/the-campaign
5   https://www.news18.com/sports/indian-paralympic-success-largest-ever-contingent-top-training-and-foreign-exposure-like-olympic-contingent-pm-modis-support-9036961.html

Going the Last Mile

1   https://gco.iarc.who.int/media/globocan/factsheets/populations/356-india-fact-sheet.pdf
2   https://www.denvaxindia.com/news

Let the Amrit Kaal Be a Buildathon

1 https://www.sae.org/binaries/content/assets/cm/content/attend/2018/student-events/aero-design-west/results/2014west_micro.pdf

2 https://www.sae.org/binaries/content/assets/cm/content/attend/2018/student-events/aero-design-east/results/2015_east_final.pdf

3 Sachar Committee Report (2006)

Reflections of a Diplomat

1 The Supreme Court in Special Leave Petition (Civil) No.28609 of 2011 vide its Order dated 08.05.2012 and 13.04.2013, inter-alia, observed that Haj subsidy be done away with and directed the Central Government to progressively reduce the amount of subsidy so as to completely eliminate the same within a period of 10 years. https://indiankanoon.org/doc/124837377/?type=print

2 Om Marathe, '*Explained: Aden, the war-torn Yemeni port's deep India connections*', Indian Express, 14 August 2019, https://indianexpress.com/article/explained/aden-the-war-torn-yemeni-ports-deep-india-connections-5904398/

3 https://www.mea.gov.in/images/pdf/pr-dep-yemen.pdf

4 https://timesofindia.indiatimes.com/city/pune/freedom-fighter-vasudev-phadkes-memorial-gets-new-lease-of-life/articleshow/104979133.cms

5 K. Spynk, *Mother Teresa: An authorized biography* (Harper One, 1997), pp. 166-67

6 E.M. Stone, '*Mother Teresa: A life of love*' (Paulist Press, 1999), pp.68-70.

7   https://www.illinois.gov/news/press-release.13860.html
8   https://indiapost.com/maharashtra-cm-leads-top-trade-team-to-michigan/
9   https://timesofindia.indiatimes.com/city/chandigarh/haryana-ties-up-with-iowa-for-fruit-techs/articleshow/53731295.cms

Bridging Worlds: My Journey as an Indian Muslim Scholar in International Relations

1   https://www.mea.gov.in/Speeches-Statements.htm?dtl/34713
2   https://www.mea.gov.in/press-releases.htm?dtl/38161/The_3rd_Voice_of_Global_South_Summit_2024 (See also G. Sachdeva, 'India as the Voice of the Global South in G20, 2023.', *Indian Foreign Affairs Journal*, 17(3/4) (2022): 133–45. https://www.jstor.org/stable/48772505. Accessed 15 Aug. 2024.)
3   'Literacy Rate among Minorities', Government of India Press Information Bureau, 10 February 2022, https://www.pib.gov.in/PressReleasePage.aspx?PRID=1797310
4   Sachar Committee Report (2006), see Section 4.1 and Figures 5.3 and 5.4.
5   C-01: 'Population by religious community, India – 2011', Government of India Census Digital Library, https://censusindia.gov.in/nada/index.php/catalog/11361

A People's General

1   https://www.ndtv.com/india-news/no-incident-of-stone-pelting-took-place-in-jammu-and-kashmir-in-2023-says-amit-shah-4969302

2   S. A. Hasnain, 'The 'missing' muslim regiment: Without comprehensive rebuttal, Pakistani propaganda dupes the gullible across the board', *Times of India*, 29 November 2017. https://timesofindia.indiatimes.com/ blogs/toi-edit-page/the-missing-muslim-regiment-without-comprehensive-rebuttal-pakistani-propaganda-dupes-the-gullible-across-the-board/

Faith in Constitutional Ideas Is the Only Way Out

1   As per the All India Survey on Higher Education (AISHE), 2021-22 report, the total enrolment in higher education is 4.33 crore (p. i), while Muslim enrolment is 21.1 Lakh (p. 40). This is a 4.87 per cent representation. See full report here: https://cdnbbsr. s3waas.gov.in/s392049debbe566ca5782a3045cf300a3c/ uploads/2024/02/20240719952688509.pdf   or   here: https://aishe.gov.in/

2   The AISHE 2021-22 report notes that Muslim women's enrolment in higher education is 10.4 lakh, up from 8.98 lakh in 2017-18 (p. 40).

3   D. Lelyveld, *Aligarh's first generation : Muslim solidarity in British India* (Princeton, N.J. : Princeton University Press, 1978), pp. 130-132. (See also A. M. Khan, '*How the clergy wanted Sir Syed beheaded*', Times of India, 19 Oct 2009, https://timesofindia.indiatimes.com/india/how-the-clergy-wanted-sir-syed-beheaded/articleshow/5137469.cms)

4   The Supreme Court in St. Stephens College v. University of Delhi (1992 AIR 1630) ruled that minority institutions can reserve up to 50 per cent of seats for members of their own community, and shall make available at least 50 per cent of the annual admission to members of communities other

than the minority community. The admission of other community candidates shall be done purely on the basis of merit.

5   See https://economictimes.indiatimes.com/news/politics-and-nation/supreme-court-calls-triple-talaq-sinful-but-reserves-verdict-on-validity/articleshow/58736718.cms?from=mdr for instance.

6   F. Mustafa, 'No instant solution yet', The Tribune, 31 Aug 2017, https://www.tribuneindia.com/news/archive/comment/no-instant-solution-yet-459700

Why Prime Minister Narendra Modi Is My Role Model

1   'Pradhan Mantri Garib Kalyan Package', National Portal of India, https://www.india.gov.in/spotlight/pradhan-mantri-garib-kalyan-package-pmgkp

2   'Free Foodgrains for 81.35 crore beneficiaries for five years: Cabinet Decision', Government of India Press Information Bureau, 29 November 2023, https://pib.gov.in/PressReleasePage.aspx?PRID=1980686

3   For a detailed discussion on this, see T. Ahmad, (2021) 'The Paint of Muslim Society: Population, Politics, and Reservation', *Islam and Muslim Societies: A Social Science Journal*, 14(2): 48-50. Available at https://www.muslimsocieties.org/wp-content/uploads/2022/03/The-Paint-of-Muslim-Society-Population-Politics-and-Reservation.pdf

For the Love of the Land

1   https://pib.gov.in/PressReleaseIframePage.aspx?PRID=1797158

2   A.M. Rizvi (2010). Islamic Environmental Ethics and the Challenge of Anthropocentrism. *American Journal of Islam and Society*, 27(3): 53–78. https://doi.org/10.35632/ajis.v27i3.366

3   https://bliis.org/essay/planting-a-tree-in-the-end-times-an-analysis-of-an-islamic-and-jewish-saying/

4   https://aboutislam.net/reading-islam/about-muhammad/prophet-muhammad-pioneer-environment/

5   "[The University of Maryland's Global Terrorism Database II] recorded 7,184 terrorist incidents between 1998 and 2004. The largest number of terrorist incidents occurred in India (784)." This means that 10 per cent of all globally recorded terrorist attacks between 1998 and 2004 took place in India, well after the militancy had peaked in Jammu & Kashmir. It represents an average of 130 terrorist attacks a year, averaging to about one every 3 days. "In terms of terrorist-related fatalities, India (3,008 deaths) again headed the list of countries" V.K. Borooah, 'Terrorist Incidents in India, 1998–2004: A Quantitative Analysis of Fatality Rates.', *Terrorism and Political Violence*, 21(3): 476–498. https://doi.org/10.1080/09546550902970165 {Note: The SATP figures are much higher. See next endnote}

6   https://satp.org/datasheet-terrorist-attack/incidents-data/india

Change Doesn't Stop Because a Theory Says It Is Impossible

1   IANS, 'Shivjyoti Rajput's 'JNU: Jahangir National University' Role Inspired By Shehla Rashid', Outlook, 01 April 2024 https://www.outlookindia.com/art-

entertainment/shivjyoti-rajputs-jnu-jahangir-national-university-role-inspired-by-shehla-rashid

2   https://iep.utm.edu/rene-descartes/#SH4a

3   https://plato.stanford.edu/entries/descartes/

4   Isaac Newton's primary objective in writing the Principia Mathematica was to demonstrate that the laws governing the universe reflected intelligent design. He explicitly expressed this aim in correspondence with Richard Bentley, stating that his intent was to provide evidence supporting the existence of a divine creator. https://www.newtonproject.ox.ac.uk/view/texts/normalized/THEM00254

5   'With the establishment of a relationship of oppression, violence has already begun. Never in history has violence been initiated by the oppressed. How could they be the initiators, if they themselves are the result of violence? How could they be the sponsors of something whose objective inauguration called forth their existence as oppressed? There would be no oppressed had there been no prior situation of violence to establish their subjugation.' From Paulo Freire, *Pedagogy of the Oppressed* (New York, London: Continuum, 2005), https://envs.ucsc.edu/internships/internship-readings/freire-pedagogy-of-the-oppressed.pdf

6   Sachar Committee Report (2006), p. 107.

7   Sachar Committee Report (2006), p. 108.

8   Ava Kofman, 'Bruno Latour, the Post-Truth Philosopher, Mounts a Defense of Science', The *New York Times Magazine*, 25 October 2018, https://www.nytimes.com/2018/10/25/magazine/bruno-latour-post-truth-philosopher-science.html

Perspectives on Deprivation, Victimhood Narrative, Isolationism and Radicalization

1   Sachar Committee Report (2006), pp. 13-15.

2   Sachar Committee Report (2006).

3   Sachar Committee Report (2006) pp. 15-16.

4   Sachar Committee Report (2006), p. 107.

5   O. Lewis, 'The culture of poverty', *Society* 35(2) (1998): 7–9.

6   R.T. Kiyosaki, *Rich Dad Poor Dad*. (2nd ed.) (Scottsdale, AZ: Plata Publishing, 2017).

7   C-09: 'Educational level by religious community and sex for population age 7 and above, 2011', Government of India Census Digital Library, https://censusindia.gov.in/nada/index.php/catalog/2493

8   M. Ismail, A.A. Shah, K. Saleem & A. Khan (2020). Why educated youth inclined toward extremism: A case of higher education institutes of Pakistan. *Asian Journal of Comparative Politics*, 7(3): 419-434. https://doi.org/10.1177/2057891120926567

9   https://quran.com/13/11

10 Hillel Ofek, 'Why the Arabic World Turned Away from Science', *The New Atlantis*, Number 30, Winter 2011, pp. 3-23. https://www.thenewatlantis.com/publications/why-the-arabic-world-turned-away-from-science

11 https://www.aljazeera.com/news/2021/6/1/saudi-minister-defends-volume-limit-on-mosque-loudspeakers

12 https://gulfnews.com/uae/dh500-fine-for-stopping-vehicles-to-pray-on-roadside-1.2110833

13 https://www.independent.co.uk/news/world/middle-east/saudi-arabia-declares-all-atheists-are-terrorists-in-new-law-to-crack-down-on-political-dissidents-9228389.html

14 "Between 1951 and 2011, Muslims grew by 4.4 percentage
    points to 14.2% of the population, while Hindus declined
    by 4.3 points to 79.8%." https://www.pewresearch.org/
    religion/2021/09/21/population-growth-and-religious-
    composition/

15 For a detailed discussion on this, see T. Ahmad, 'The Paint
    of Muslim Society: Population, Politics, and Reservation',
    Islam and Muslim Societies: A Social Science Journal,
    14(2): 48-50. Available at https://www.muslimsocieties.
    org/wp-content/uploads/2022/03/The-Paint-of-Muslim-
    Society-Population-Politics-and-Reservation.pdf

Scan QR code to access the
Penguin Random House India website